SELL UNAFRAID

SELL UNAFRAID

Unleash Sales Success Through Personal Discipline

Tom Reber

Published by Game Changer Publishing

Paperback ISBN: 978-1-963793-14-7

Hardcover ISBN: 978-1-963793-15-4

Digital: ISBN: 978-1-963793-16-1

GC GAME CHANGER
PUBLISHING
www.GameChangerPublishing.com

DEDICATION

To all those committed to demolishing mediocrity
and bringing their best to each day.

STOP RIGHT THERE

Before you dive in, you're gonna see a few spots throughout the book that mention some bonus resources. This is my gift to help YOU get the winning edge so you can *Sell Unfraid.*

Go ahead and claim these resources NOW before you get started.

SELL UNAFRAID

UNLEASH SALES SUCCESS THROUGH PERSONAL DISCIPLINE

TOM REBER

FOREWORD

Our lives are often defined more by a series of small thoughts and actions instead of a single significant event that changes our lives. When it comes to sales, the thoughts that become ACTION are everything.

The faster the world moves, the more opportunities we encounter. Each creates the possibility of moving forward in the direction we've imagined for ourselves when we approach them the right way to sell and grow our businesses and lives.

That's why *SELL UNAFRAID* is as important as ever and a book the world needed written by a man built to deliver the message.

My friend Tom has crafted a book that is both timely and packed with timeless advice you can use every day to live the best life you've imagined for yourself to drive GROWTH. *SELL UNAFRAID* is a revealing exploration of Tom's hard-earned wisdom and valuable life lessons that will fortify your mental and financial bottom lines, leading you to a happier and more peaceful existence.

SELL UNAFRAID celebrates Tom's important work of helping people who work with their hands to keep working with their brains, as well as impacting people across all industries. Tom's lifelong mission and this landmark book continue that calling while also spelling out tactics and the mindset you need to do better in life, no matter your profession or vocation.

I'm also honored and humbled to contribute to Tom's book because we share what I call the Prizefighter Days mentality. We both believe in optimizing your physical and mental abilities, winning one day at a time, staying focused on what you can control, and stacking your wins one on top of another. Because at the end of the day, to WIN more takes daily discipline. *SELL UNAFRAID* is an affirmation of these proven strategies Tom has successfully used for years.

Now he is sharing them with you to help you win your battles, too, and sell more.

If you're ready to transform your life and business and ATTACK GROWTH, turn the page and start your journey to see how *SELL UNAFRAID* can help you live the life you've always imagined for yourself.

—Ben Newman
USA Today TOP 5 Performance Coach in World
2X *Wall Street Journal* Bestselling Author

CONTENTS

INTRODUCTION
SALESPEOPLE SUCK

He pulled up on a Saturday morning, walked up my driveway, and knocked on the door at the scheduled time.

Good start, I thought.

My wife Lee welcomed the sales guy into our home. He introduced himself and began with the typical pleasantries. Somehow, before we moved to the area of the house where we needed work done, he started telling us about his daughter and her volleyball travel team. He then moved on to the topic of his restored classic car and something about his fiancé.

I admit that, while he was barfing all of this onto us, I thought: *I don't give a shit*.

We were converting part of our basement into my content production space and had big plans. I had about 1,000 square feet to work with, and this new floor would lay the foundation for everything else. I knew I wanted some kind of concrete stain or epoxy to replace the carpet. The gray/black finish would look great with the other things Lee had in mind since she was designing it all.

We left our foyer and made our way down the basement steps, where he asked, "What do you want done?"

I started with how I wanted an epoxy floor...

"No, you don't!" interrupted Mr. Sales Guy. "You want the X5P3000"—or whatever he said—"floor finish."

For the next ten minutes, he told us all the technical reasons we wanted this finish. He bragged about how many floors they'd done. He went on and on about things we didn't care about.

At one point, Lee asked him, "What's this going to cost?"

"It's going to be *a lot* of money," he shot back.

"A lot?" I echoed.

"Probably $9,000–$10,000 for this." He paused momentarily. "But we're really good at this. We do hundreds of jobs a year and have great reviews."

I said we'd get back to him because that's what prospects do when they want to lie to a salesperson.

We escorted him out the door. As it closed, Lee turned and said to me with frustration, "I know about his daughter and her volleyball, his fiancée and the car he restored—and he doesn't know a fucking thing about me."

On to the next company.

I'll pick this story up later in the book and share what would've made us sign a contract and cut a check on the spot.

The typical sales experience leaves many unimpressed. In any industry composed mainly of small businesses, salespeople usually lack energy, empathy, training, and the proper mindset to perform at an elite level. These shortcomings are responsible for sales targets not being met and anorexic profits.

About 99.9% of businesses in the United States are small business-es.[1] That's about 33 million of them. A small business is generally defined as one that is independently owned and operated, employs fewer than 100 employees, and makes less than $10 million in annual revenue.

If you picked up this book, there's a great chance that you fall into this category. This book is for you.

This book is especially for you if you're a home improvement contractor. The stats I'm sharing with you are counting all business categories, but I believe the numbers are worse for the contracting

---

1. According to a *Forbes* article dated December of 2022.

space. There are over 3.6 million "contractors" in the United States. Less than 5% hit $500k in topline revenue. Less than 10% hit one million. We can do better.

Research will also show you that 50% of small businesses fail within the first five years of opening their doors.[2] They fail because they don't consistently sell enough volume at the profit margins needed to survive. Moreover, the majority of the other half live with unhealthy amounts of stress. Most lack money and barely scrape by. This lack of money causes them to work more. This hard work, done with the best of intentions, creates a life where, instead of providing for our families and building a stronger future, we end up stealing time, money, and memories from them. We become slaves to the business.

The pressure to win is a heavy load on the small business owner.

Small businesses with sales teams are under the same pressures. Less than 50% of salespeople hit their targets. Consider your team of six that you employ to sell your stuff at the right profit margins: at least three of them aren't performing as needed. This hurts the business and the salesperson, impacting their chance of reaching their financial goals.

Salespeople suck.

Not because they're bad people—though let's be real, some of them flat-out embarrass the profession with shady, slimy crap that makes the rest of us look bad.

Not because they're not trying. Most want to do well and put in some effort.

Most drop the ball in simple ways. This is due to a lack of training and accountability. It's due to not knowing how to protect their time, show up with confidence, and live to a daily code geared toward performing at elite levels.

Another reason salespeople struggle is because we play the same game as all the other salespeople. We agree to play by the rules the prospect lays out, which doesn't serve us. For instance, many years ago, I had this waste of time sales call.

It was a Saturday morning—normally pancakes, cartoons, and

---

2. Shane, S.A., 2008. *The illusions of entrepreneurship: The costly myths that entrepreneurs, investors, and policy makers live by.* Yale University Press.

family time. But nope. There I was, suiting up for a sales appointment that had the nerve to lock in at 9 a.m. Sharp. The prospect's "only time"—like their schedule was gospel and mine didn't matter. And what did I do? I caved. Said yes. All in the name of chasing a deal and providing for my family. That decision cost me the chance to show up for my son's basketball game. That stung. It was a moment where I chose someone else's priorities over my own—and it pissed me off.

En route, I got my mind right, and my enthusiasm was on fire. A $35-50k whole-house paint job awaited, and the weather joined the party, with the sun shining and perfect temperatures. I figured this was a slam dunk due to the golden ticket that got me in the door—a referral.

I'll keep the rest of the story short since I tell it fully in my first book, *Winning the Contractor Fight*. The homeowner scheduled a total of eight of us to walk the property and compete for the work. The following Wednesday, after I'd spent about ten hours putting the proposal together, including revisions, breakdowns, and answering multiple questions, I heard, "We're going with someone else."

It was one of many gut punches I had taken because my sales process was broken. I chose to play by someone else's rules instead of creating and following a process based on my own.

Most salespeople suck because they settle for mediocrity. If you're reading this, I believe you're interested in performing at higher levels. You have an expectation of yourself or your team to consistently perform at elite levels in your sales game. You want to be respected, and you want to protect your time.

This book will open your eyes and challenge you. It will also, from time to time, cause you to ask, "This is so basic; where's the advanced stuff?" In those moments, I ask you to lean in and pay more attention because there's gold there. Most overlook the basics. Don't make the same mistake.

SELL UNAFRAID: Unleash Sales Success Through Personal Discipline comprises four main sections, each of a few chapters. Section 1 is about winning with your mindset. The life you want—the income, the house, the freedom—all start with growing a stronger you.

Section 2 is about selling more of your stuff. This section is about how to bring the sale home in an empathetic and ethical way where everyone wins.

In Section 3, I dig into The Hunt. Most small business salespeople and owners do very little to prospect for business. In this section, I'll share some strategies that have earned me millions of dollars. Prospecting doesn't need to be scary or something you avoid, like a colonoscopy. This section will add 20%–50% more to your revenue when implemented consistently.

Finally, Section 4 is about what happens after you make the sale. Most contractor salespeople "close" the deal and skip out like it was a one-night stand. I will show you how to keep the love burning hot long after the final check is cashed.

SELL UNAFRAID will help you overcome your negative self-talk about selling. It will equip you to solve more problems for your clients and make their lives easier. It will show you how to differentiate in a world full of mediocre salespeople. Never forget, that differentiation is crucial to selling more at higher profits.

Before we dig in, I also want to share what you won't find in this book. First, you won't read anything that isn't a proven strategy, tactic, or framework for success. Nothing in here is theory. Everything you read in this book is something that is being done by me or my team, something I've personally done in the past, or something that I (in my businesses, Simplify Painting & The Contractor Fight) and our clients are actually doing now to sell more.

Second, you won't find a list of "They say this, you say that" sales scripts. While I believe word tracks or scripts can be helpful for a sales-person, this book will instead focus on giving you frameworks to filter your unique situation through. I want you to take what you read and make it your own. You'll get more from the frameworks than if I gave you a paint-by-numbers approach. I want you to learn to be critical, creative, and disciplined within your own context.

Selling Unafraid isn't about puffing out your chest or playing the tough-guy sales game. Forget that bro-culture garbage—no one's impressed. This is about real courage and unshakable discipline. It's about living by a personal code that doesn't bend, doesn't flinch, and doesn't make excuses. It's showing up like a pro, day in and day out, no matter what the scoreboard says. It's having the guts to prepare when no one's watching, to sharpen your sword before you step into battle. Selling Unafraid isn't about fancy scripts or slick closing lines. Those are worthless if you don't have the discipline to do the work and the balls to stand by your code when it's hard.

I'm tired of mediocre, untrained, uncaring, unreliable salespeople. I wrote this book to unfuck the situation.

PART 1
PREPARE

CHAPTER 1
SUCCESS IS AN INSIDE-OUT GAME

Success doesn't start with your business plan, your sales pitch, or your marketing strategy. It starts with you. Inside you. How you think, how you act, how you show up for yourself—that's the foundation. Period.

I've been very physically active in my life. As a United States Marine and an athlete, keeping my machine in tune has always been important. However, several years ago, I started to put my health on the back burner, all in the name of building my companies and taking care of my family. I did a good job at providing. I worked my ass and enjoyed a decent level of success. Even though I was in fairly good shape, I lacked confidence. I knew I could be better. In February of 2022, I was challenged to get my ass in gear and get serious about my health.

I had fallen prey to the mindset of "pretty good for…"

"I'm in pretty good shape for a 50-year-old."

"I'm pretty disciplined for someone who has so much going on."

Pretty good for…

Mediocrity had burrowed its way into me and cloaked itself in excuses. The justifications I was making were keeping me from experiencing greater victories in every area of my life. True success demands our best, not just "pretty good for."

The success you want as a salesperson begins with respect for yourself. It's crazy to see someone eating like crap, drinking too much, not exercising, and neglecting sleep, yet thinking they will be a high-performing sales machine. As the saying goes, "How you do one thing is how you do everything." If you're a slob personally, you'll be a slob professionally.

Your sales career will be as strong as you are. This is why I speak so much about taking care of your mind, body, and soul—aka "Get Oxygen." Sales is a demanding profession. It requires mental toughness, confidence, energy, and stamina. Being an elite salesperson requires uncommon mental clarity and emotional intelligence. Show me someone who takes their self-discipline lightly, and I'll show you an underperforming salesperson.

Some people try to justify their lack of self-respect and discipline by saying, "I hit my sales targets, so it's not affecting my career." I'm pretty good for…

Hitting your targets and showing up as your best are not the same thing. Those who don't take care of the machine are leaving money on the table.

You are the first domino on the way to exceptional sales success. When you choose to feed yourself first, everything else is more likely to fall into place.

When I speak to groups about this, I draw a circle and write "YOU" in the center. Then, I draw another circle around the first one, and inside it I write "HOME." Finally, I draw a third circle, in which I write "BUSINESS." This is what I mean when I say success is an inside-out game. There is a hierarchy to earning long-lasting success in anything, especially sales.

Take care of yourself first, then your loved ones at home, and finally, your career. Sadly, many people put their careers first and give themselves and their loved ones their scraps, which in turn affects their sales results.

A few years ago, my wife stood on the stage in front of over 400 people attending our event and dropped the key to winning in business:

"Success starts at home."

These words have echoed within our community for several years.

Its very simplicity means it's often overlooked in the quest for more advanced strategies and tactics.

Of course, winning in business does require the right strategies, plans, and tactics. You can't win without a great plan of attack! But many people lack a strong foundation, built from the inside out, on which their companies or careers can stand.

Work on yourself.

Build a strong home life.

Dominate your business.

In that order.

Let's get back to me and my battle with mediocrity.

I accepted the challenge to work on myself, and in February 2022, I began a program called 75 Hard. The program consists of six guidelines that participants are expected to adhere to continuously for 75 days, aiming to enhance their fitness, health, and mental resilience.

For those thinking, *Wait! I thought I was reading a book on sales. What's with all this fitness stuff?* I ask you to hang with me. A strong you is the foundation for strong and consistent sales.

75 Hard is a mental toughness program. It's designed to make you uncomfortable and prove to yourself that you have what it takes to battle through adversity and inconvenience. Fitness is just one aspect of the program.

I was feeling numb, going through the motions of life and business. My mind felt cluttered, and my body was getting soft. I didn't like what I saw in the mirror. I knew it wasn't really who I wanted to be. Deep down, the truth stung. I was undisciplined, and I hated a little of myself for it.

The good news was that this was within my control. I had made decisions that compounded over time, putting me exactly where I was.

So, on February 23, 2022, I began the program created by entrepreneur Andy Frisella. Millions of people have begun this free program. Many fewer have finished on their first attempt. Many others have finished after a few tries.

The requirement is 75 days in a row with zero deviation. There is no one to report to. This is 100% on the honor system. If you fail at one task at any point, you go back to Day 1.

This is a great place to kickstart your mental toughness. It requires you to improve the skills that will build your personal discipline. It will require you to silence the "bitch voice" inside you that makes excuses about why you can't see something through. The program is inconvenient. It's supposed to be hard.

For example, when I would travel, I knew getting two workouts in would be tough, especially with time zone differences. I would do my first workout of the day at 00:01 a.m. I'd shower and climb into bed. Then, I'd get up and catch my 7:00 a.m. flight, and whenever I landed and traveled to my hotel, I would immediately do my second workout. Non-negotiable. This sucked. It inconvenienced not only me but also the people I was traveling with. I'd sometimes leave a business dinner early or arrive a bit late because I had to get the second workout in.

How many people use travel as an excuse for not following through on a commitment? How many blame the next holiday, birthday, or work party for why they don't want to commit to something good for them?

Right about the time I was settling into my groove and sprinting toward the finish line of my first round of 75 Hard, I put on my 60-pound weighted vest for my second workout of the day. It was March 31st, around noon. Half an hour into the workout, my left foot popped. I didn't just feel it, I heard it.

My foot was broken on day thirty-seven of the program. I was done. I needed to heal up for several weeks and give it another shot when I was able to.

Just kidding. That's what most people would've done. A convenient excuse to tap out had presented itself. This is where most people let themselves off the hook. The world will tell you it's ok to stop the program. "You broke your foot! You need to heal up," they'll say. "You need to rest," they'll insist. "You can't do it all," they'll argue.

They will say anything to let you off the hook so they don't feel pressure to raise their own standards.

Let's also get some perspective here: it's just a broken foot. There are far worse things that could have hit me. This was only my foot. If we tap out when the small things come, what will happen when bigger challenges show up? Each day, each moment, we all have an opportunity to grow stronger. Keep stacking those wins.

What "broken foot" excuses have you used to lapse from a consistent code in your life? Did you go bankrupt? Okay, get some perspective, be grateful for the lessons you learned through that, and make different choices. Your relationship ended with someone you loved? That sucks – or maybe it will turn out to be the best thing that ever happened to you. Adversity striking is not a hall pass to blow off the commitments we've made. Time will still pass. Who do you want to be on the other side of your "broken foot"?

Back to the moment my foot went *"crack."* My first thought was, *Shit. Now I need to modify my workouts.* I finished the workout and dragged myself another half mile to my house.

As I walked in the door, The Queen said, "What happened?"

I told her I thought I'd broken it and needed to go to urgent care.

Her first words were, "Well, looks like you'll be doing a lot more sit-ups in your workouts."

Truth. There were plenty of things I was able to do no matter what was going on with my foot.

My 75 Hard experiences took me to a new level of focus and discipline. My mental clarity was off the charts. I felt like I could see around corners. I was sharp. My confidence grew by the minute. My business grew. My bank account grew. My relationship with Lee grew. I got in amazing shape and dropped about 25 pounds.

I recommend 75 Hard to everyone I talk to.

SUCCESS DOESN'T CARE HOW YOU FEEL

It didn't matter that I broke my foot. It didn't matter if I had to travel. Success takes what it takes, and the number one reason most people don't achieve their goals is they continue to cave to their feelings. About 75% of salespeople across all industries fail to hit their sales goals.[1] I believe this is due to caving to how they feel instead of honoring a personal code of conduct.

1. Based on data collected by the Objective Management Group from about 650,000 people (https://www.objectivemanagement.com/).

The average person looks for ways out of discomfort and inconvenience. The exceptional person embraces the hard way and welcomes the challenge. The exceptional person sees adversity as an opportunity to grow.

Starting 75 Hard was easy. The challenge of the program lies in dozens of micro-decisions each day: "Will I do what I said I'd do, or not?" Success in sales is tightly related to your confidence level. Want more confidence? Honor the commitments you make to yourself.

YOUR LAST 30 DAYS

Let's look back over the past month of your life. Pick an area of life that you say is important to you and where you want to achieve more.

How did you do? The daily actions you committed to—what was your record?

Did you commit to five crucial actions each day? Did you go 5–0, 2–3, or 1–4?

The only acceptable answer is 5–0.

Before you start arguing with me in your head about how "nobody's perfect" and all that BS, let's get some perspective.

Your actions are your choice. The commitments you made were made by *you*! If that's the case, why would you not perform flawlessly in something you yourself set up? You set the rules and are in complete control of your choices.

On the very rare occasions you do not go 5–0 in the actions required for success, the only acceptable reason is that something catastrophic has prevented you from following your own rule.

Back to your last 30 days:

- You said you'd make five cold calls a day...
- You promised to stick to a specific diet...
- You pledged to eat dinner as a family at 6:00 p.m. every night...

How'd you do?

"The success you want doesn't care how you feel.
The kick-ass future version of you is counting on
you to win the current moments today."

Pick one thing today and commit to going undefeated. This will send a message to yourself that you have what it takes to live and perform at an elite level.

Isn't that why you picked up a copy of this book—to be an elite salesperson?

A strong you is the foundation of the success you want in sales. Mental toughness is required to handle adversity, negative self-talk, and the challenges in the economy you will face in your sales career.

How you do one thing is how you do everything.

Choosing to live by your own high-level code will carry over into honoring the work required to *SELL UNAFRAID*.

Living by your non-negotiable code develops confidence. Confidence is key to sales success. Confidence is attractive. It draws others to you. A confident *you* guarantees greater sales success.

I know that you have greatness in you. You have what it takes to earn more. You have what it takes to fulfill the dreams you have for your family and to build your legacy.

Success is an inside-out game.

You are the center of all the success you want.

CHAPTER 2
WIN THE MOMENTS

MACRO & MICRO DECISIONS

Success is simple when you understand the difference between macro and micro decisions. Making the choice to lose 20 pounds in the next 90 days is a macro decision. Choosing to honor the eating plan you committed to, or going to the gym at the planned time, are micro decisions made in the moment.

Choosing to increase your sales by $1,000,000 in the next year is also a macro decision. The daily activities that will earn that million bucks are micro decisions.

You can't just make a macro decision at a moment in time and expect things to fall into place. Every day is an opportunity to prove to yourself and others that you're serious about the goal you set.

If you've consistently achieved the goals you have set, you have a winning record when it comes to micro-decisions. If you habitually don't achieve your goals, you're losing the micro-decision battles you face each day.

I have a client named Bob who runs a General Contracting business. In the past twelve months, he has personally added over one million dollars in revenue to his company. This is in addition to the other couple million his team has sold. Bob has battled through a ton of adversity and distractions. They're many of the same ones you have: employees being knuckleheads, making payroll, COVID, clients changing timelines on projects, etc. There have also been some good distractions, like adding a couple of kids to the family over the past three years!

Bob had gotten to a point where it was easy to see nothing but the problems in the business. Have you been there? All you can see are the challenges that slap you in the face each day. It can cause you to become cynical of everyone and jaded about any initiative you've committed to. To his credit, Bob chose to do something about it. He was tired of being mad, tired of his team underperforming, tired of settling. He chose to be the example and create momentum.

We teach thousands of people what winning the moments looks like, and yet only a small percentage achieve the results Bob does. Is it the training? Is it where they live? The industry they're in?

None of the above.

The additional one million he generated is the result of him choosing to win the moments throughout each day and doing what he committed to doing. Bob chooses to win the days. He understands that to win a day, he needs to win the moments that make up the day. He is consistent. He wins the micro-decisions more days than others. He faces the same distractions as we all do—the same fires to put out, the stress, the fatigue, and the occasional "I just don't feel like doing it." Bob simply wins more moments than he loses.

Take a minute and think about a goal you've set for yourself that you're having a tough time achieving. How have you shown up in that area of life in the last thirty days? Are you relentless about winning the micro-decision moments, or have you too often tapped out for whatever reason that seemed important at the time?

You're not losing weight?

Your sales have stalled?

You're not winning the moment.

Success is really this simple: Win the Moments You Have Control Over.

If you want to win at higher levels in any area of your life—this is the foundation of your success.

Call the pissed-off customer back—now. *Right this moment.* Do it before the negativity compounds and the consequences grow.

You have five minutes before lunch and another prospect to call. Win *this* moment and call them *now.* Choose not to put it off until after lunch.

> *"Time kills deals.*
> *Make sure it's not you doing the killing."*

You made a commitment to do a sales role-play today: be there. Be all-in. Put in the work and get 1% better today.

Momentum is a game-changer.

Action leads to more action. When you choose to win this moment, it creates momentum toward the next. Each time we make a choice to lose a moment, the train stops and more effort is required to get it moving again.

Most salespeople hate prospecting. Why wouldn't they? It's hard to hear "no" all day. Going into someone's office or picking up the phone to create a sales opportunity is exhausting, and on top of that, they don't want to talk to you! So, we don't do it. We negotiate with ourselves and weasel out of it with some BS excuse. Or if we do it, we don't bring our best to the task at hand.

In 2004, I set a goal to sell our painting services to a well-known and successful homebuilder in our area. This account would change our business and move me closer to building the company I envisioned.

I walked into their office with my fancy company folder and marketing materials, asking the older woman behind the desk if I could talk to someone about bidding on their work.

Her reply was unforgettable: "Albert has been our painter for 20 years, and the only way anyone else is getting a shot is if he dies."

Disappointed, I thanked her, left my folder, and went on my way.

A couple of days later, I saw one of their job sites and decided to win the moment. I stopped and left a card with one of their people, then continued on my way.

A few weeks later, as I drove near their office, I stopped in and approached the woman behind the desk, who seemed less than thrilled to see me.

"Hi. I was just stopping by to see if Albert had died yet."

She chuckled and said no. I left another folder.

This dance continued for a little over fourteen months.

I'd see their trucks, and I'd stop and say hi.

I was near their office: try again.

If I saw they were developing a new community, I'd send an email about it.

"Did he die yet?"

"No. Go away."

Even though I saw zero results, I was building momentum. I became like a persistent rash that refused to go away. I chose to do my part: to win the moments. This momentum carried over into how I approached every day, and prospecting became my strength. During those fourteen months of striking out with them, I picked up several other general contractors and builders, and our sales grew. How you do one thing is how you do everything.

On December 26, 2005, while taking a few days off for Christmas, my phone rang. It was Mike, one of the superintendents for my dream client. He shared that Albert had pissed him off one too many times. He vented his frustrations, mentioning how they had become complacent and were dropping the ball.

"I'm calling because I've seen your materials around the office, and I need a new painter."

The following week, I met with Mike and the other three superintendents. We connected and discussed what the ideal relationship would look like. They toured some of our other projects and shortly after awarded us our first of many jobs. Overnight, this account added about $500,000 to our annual revenue.

What would have happened if I hadn't chosen to win the moments and create momentum? Was it discipline or the perfect sales language that won the sale?

Many salespeople fail to understand that the small and consistent actions required for success often don't produce visible results immediately. These moments are compounding. Take bamboo, for example. It takes five years to grow. It needs to be consistently watered and fertilized where it was planted. For more than four years, there are no visible signs of growth. Then, in year five, in a five-week period, the bamboo shoots up to around ninety feet!

Many things affect sales results. One of them is timing. People buy when they're ready, not when we're ready. Our job is to keep showing up and winning the moments. In due time, when the prospect is ready, you'll get your opportunity.

Your job is simple: take the actions you have control over every day.

If you're leading a sales team, this is your management tool. Yes, you should keep score and track sales, profits, and other key performance indicators. (We'll explore this in more detail in the next chapter.) But for now, establish the non-negotiable daily actions that, when honored, will lead to the sales success you want.

In my sales workshops, one of the biggest complaints I hear from leaders is that they don't know how their salespeople are spending their time. This is a coaching opportunity within your company. Sit down and map out the actions you expect from your team on a daily basis. Coach them on how to set up their week for success. Have them report on these activities weekly in your sales meetings. What we focus on improves. In football, the goal is to get the ball across the goal line. A good coach will focus on getting first downs. As you move the chains, you're more likely to score points.

Define what those first downs look like with your sales team. Measure, coach, and expect them to do their part.

This is how you win the sales game.

CHAPTER 3
MINDSETS OF ELITE PERFORMANCE

"Elite salespeople have a secret weapon. It's not the words they say.
It's not the quality of leads they get.
It's not something they're born with. It's discipline."

They choose to show up with consistency every day in the areas that will move them closer to their goals. Most salespeople, the average ones, choose to base their actions on their feelings or on the circumstances that are presented.

So, what is it that the elite ones actually do more consistently than the others?

They train, track, and continually grow. They do this consistently regardless of what results they're getting. Whether they are crushing it or are in a slump, they show up consistently.

TRAIN

There are countless stories of professional athletes bringing an uncommon work ethic to their training. Tom Brady, Michael Jordan, Kobe Bryant, Walter Payton, and Jerry Rice are a few notable examples.

Even though many were blessed with God-given talent, their commitment to training is legendary. They chose not to lean on their talent or on their past success. They chose to put in massive amounts of work that would improve their skills and inspire those around them, making everyone better.

For example, Kobe was known to practice alone in a dark gym two hours before the scheduled practice or game. There's a story about him practicing from 4:15 a.m. to 11:00 a.m. because he refused to leave the gym until he made 800 shots. There are also many examples of teammates attempting to keep up with Payton or Rice during their daily hill running workouts.

The elite train daily. Professional golfers hit the range. Baseball players are in the batting cages. Professional fighters are fanatical about everything they do every day.

The elite don't only train during scheduled practices—it's a way of life. Their diet, sleep, and mental toughness practices are ingrained in their lifestyle.

James Miller, a friend and client in one of our contractor programs, BATTLEGROUND, is a testament to this. BATTLEGROUND has helped hundreds of home improvement contractors build confidence in their numbers, *SELL UNAFRAID*, and grow their brands. In 2020, on the verge of losing his home and a million bucks in debt, James chose to join the program as a last-ditch effort to turn things around. Within the program, we train contractors and their teams on how to sell. Part of this training includes daily sales role-play calls in which our members are expected to participate. James attacked it.

Every day, James was there, ready to get uncomfortable and get the reps in. For months, he got beat up in the role-plays but also continued to improve each time he stepped up to the plate. His uncommon work ethic, combined with the work he did in the unseen hours—like working on his negative self-talk and beliefs about his worth and value —created a new reality for him. Within three years, he paid off all of his debt and increased his personal income by 400%.

James is relentless. He still trains. He is constantly working on his sales game. He has changed his life forever and continues to be a stellar example for others.

The elite train.

How are you currently choosing to show up with respect to sales training? How many role-plays have you done in the last seven days? What are you feeding your mind each day?

Training is meant to be challenging. Success is difficult. The sales success you desire doesn't care how you feel about training.

I'm blown away by the number of people selling their products or services who are not actively engaged in a sales training program. Many tell me they had some sales training years ago but do nothing now. Here's the cold truth—for them, sales training is something they *did*, not something they *do*. And that's why they're broke, frustrated, and losing to guys half as talented but twice as disciplined.

In a recent sales workshop, I asked for a volunteer to role-play with me.

Crickets.

No eye contact. It was comical to watch them avoid eye contact with me!

Eventually, Mark, a young sales guy, raised his hand and said, "I'm in."

We dug in. He was shaking. Everyone in the room knew he was nervous as hell. To his credit, he persevered and was open to learning a different approach to communicating with his prospects.

Less than 24 hours later, I received a text from the owner of the company, and he was ecstatic.

"Dude! You're not going to believe this. Mark just called me and said he sold a $30,000 project using what he learned in the role-play with you!"

Training is never wasted.

There are two groups of people I want to address here.

First, if you're a salesperson, embrace training. Commit to it. Be hungry for it. If your employer refuses to provide it, then find a way to make it happen for yourself. Ensure you're ready for whatever you face when it's game time.

Next, if you're an employer and are not investing in sales training, you are doing your team, your company, yourself, and your clients a disservice. Sales training produces a 353% return on investment for the average company.[1] For every $1.00 you spend on training, you can get up to $3.53 in return. Do your job and train your team.

TRACK

In my company, The Contractor Fight, we're fanatical about a couple of metrics: email subscribers and daily revenue. In fact, every day at 8:00 a.m., a notification is posted inside our Slack account reporting on yesterday's revenue collected. Then, at 1:00 p.m., another notification reports the number of new email subscribers within the past 24 hours.

If we have a day when we have not collected money by 4:00 p.m., another notification is sent to the whole company. This alert is a GIF of SpongeBob running frantically in circles with the text "NO SALES TODAY!" flashing over and over. As of this writing (March 2024), we're at 946 days in a row of ringing the cash register. If we get the SpongeBob ALERT, the team rallies, and we find a way to generate revenue.

We track daily sales because, as we all know, nothing in a business happens without a sale. We track daily email subscribers because this drives our revenue. On average, it takes about 94 days from when someone subscribes to our list to when they spend their first dollar with us. Because of this knowledge, everything we do from a marketing perspective is designed to get someone on our email list.

Once on our list, we add value. We provide free resources, send check-in texts—whatever it takes to nurture the seeds planted. (We discuss these types of tactics in more detail later in the book.)

Success in sales is about activity. The right activities done consistently produce the revenue and profit you want. Over the past twelve years, I've worked with thousands of companies, and the majority are weak in this part of the game. Yes, most of them set a sales goal for the year, but that's where they stop. Rarely do they break these targets into quarterly, monthly, weekly, or daily activities that are tracked. For example, if our new email subscriber count is taking a hit today, we

---

1. According to a 2022 study by Task Drive; see Ostin, V., 2023. Maximizing business potential: The symbiotic relationship between employee training and business success. *Marketing Science & Inspirations*, 18(3).

know this will affect us in about 94 days if we don't make some adjustments immediately.

Do you know how many leads you need to break even? How about making a profit? Are you tracking the activities of your sales team and knowing exactly which ones yield the results you want?

Again, most set a sales goal and don't revisit it until it's too late to do anything about it. The elite sales organization keeps score. They track the number of prospecting calls made and break down the number of leads generated by source. The elite can tell you what activities produce better results and which are sabotaging their goals.

Want to *SELL UNAFRAID* and perform at elite levels? Create a culture that is fanatical about tracking.

The sky's the limit when it comes to things you can track. Take some time to identify which metrics lead to higher revenues. Focus on those and win more.

GROW

You're developing a strong you—winning the moments, and building confidence. You've been training. You're engaging in role-plays and working on developing your mindset and communication skills. You've become a tracking guru and are using that information to be more effective with your time and focus. Life is good. You even had a record sales month and received some recognition.

So what?

You're supposed to do that!

One of the major factors that keeps salespeople from achieving elite status is how they choose to show up after they win. Our tendency is to take our foot off the gas after a win. After all, we've worked hard and feel we deserve a break! After a win, it's tempting to stop doing the things that led to success in the first place. We think we've made it and no longer need to train as much or track with fanatical attention. I call this "Buying into Your Own Hype."

I believe it's actually easier to be disciplined and consistent when you're working toward building your empire or when adversity is knocking you around. We know challenging times require us to step up, fight adversity, and find a way through. My hunger to succeed was never greater than after I went bankrupt due to some poor decisions. The drive to get up and grind each day was fueled by the chip on my shoulder and my need to prove that I had what it takes to succeed at the highest levels. I've produced over 1,000 podcasts and grew The Contractor Fight to a Top 1% podcast. I've filmed over 1,500 videos on YouTube and produced over 5,000 social media posts on my way to building our brand and growing our business. Initially, many thought I was crazy because it didn't seem to be moving the needle for the first few years. They suggested I do something else. They questioned my business acumen and my understanding of what I was doing.

And who could blame the skeptics? As the content I created continued to stack, my bank account stayed the same. In fact, one year, early in the process, I only brought in a whopping $26k. I wondered if the ladder I was climbing was leaning against the right wall.

It was tough to stay focused on what I believed in at the time. Many times, I was tempted to start another business or change the direction of what I was building. There were hundreds of days filled with more doubt than belief. But I kept going because that's what you do when your back is against the wall. Or perhaps I was too stubborn to quit or too proud to concede and prove my critics right. Either way, I just did the work.

As success began to show up from my efforts, my hunger dwindled. I had recovered from the bankruptcy. I was making great money again. I was winning!

Then what?

How would I choose to show up after I was winning? This one question and my response to it has taken me and The Fight higher than I ever intended, and it will continue to do so.

Winners become addicted to the game of winning. They understand that as soon as they are satisfied with their success, mediocrity starts to creep in. How many professional athletes fizzle out after signing the big contract or being picked number one in the draft? Their hunger dissolves, and they buy into their own hype.

In the world of sales, results count. Winning matters. What impresses me most is the approach that elite salespeople take regarding their results. They strive to improve daily. They adhere to a high-level code of conduct that others are unwilling to live by. They demand the best from themselves every day and measure their performance by asking:

*"Did I show up today with my absolute best
in the areas that I control?"*

Unfortunately, we cannot make someone buy something. Sure, there are sales methods rooted in manipulation that get people to sign the contract, but the outcome of the sales appointment is beyond our control. What we do control is our mindset, thoughts, and actions. We control our preparation, our use of time, and our desire and attitude toward improvement. Through these disciplines, consistently executed, we will produce results that break records, inspire others, and change lives.

In the classic book *Good to Great*, author Jim Collins shares a couple of things I believe are relevant here:

"Good is the enemy of great."

In real life, that sounds like:

"I'm in pretty good shape for a guy in his fifties."

"I hit my sales targets, so I'm good to go."

If you're reading this book, I believe "good" was an exit you passed a long way back on your journey to greatness.

Collins also says, "Greatness is not a function of circumstance. Greatness, it turns out, is largely a matter of conscious choice and discipline."

Sounds familiar, doesn't it? *SELL UNAFRAID: Unleash Sales Success Through Personal Discipline.*

Are you courageous enough to set your sights on achieving and maintaining elite status?

I'm reminded of the old quote, "Everyone wants to be a lion until it's time to do lion shit." Chances are, you're reading this chapter and saying you want to be great and among the few elite salespeople in your industry.

"Everyone wants to be a rainmaker until it's time to do rainmaker shit."

You say you want it. Your actions will reveal whether you're for real or just another person talking shit.

CHAPTER 4

THE TRUE COST OF
MEDIOCRITY

I have personally worked with hundreds of small business owners over the past decade. They come to me with problems common to most small businesses: working crazy hours, struggling to pay the bills, and earning far less than they would if they worked for someone else. They're skilled in their craft but struggle with the money stuff. This lack of money creates other issues in their businesses, such as recruiting and retention issues, not being able to hire key players, and not having money to market their company and build their brand. This lack of money also makes people do stupid things, like borrow money and create a financial situation that can be tough to correct.

If you're reading this and thinking, *Hey, that's not me! We have constant money coming in*—hold on. I'll get to you later in this chapter.

It's common for companies to think the solution to their problems lies in creating better "systems and processes," as many business books and resources suggest, as I do as well.

"While systems are necessary for growth, most small business owners focus too much on developing these and overlook the real culprit behind their problems: Lack of Sales."

Nearly every company I have worked with faces a sales problem, even those with steady sales. I've also worked with companies that enjoy next-level profits well above their industry averages. And yes, they have a sales problem, too. They're getting passed by because they lack the discipline required to win at higher levels. In short, they're leaving money on the table.

Regardless of your current position in business, I want to highlight the cost of mediocre sales days. This one area can revive struggling businesses and elevate solid sales performers to next levels.

Anthony ran a $300,000 company as a general contractor, working tirelessly to sell his projects and support his family, which led to burnout. Within twelve months of embracing the mindset we instill in our BATTLEGROUND community—No Mediocre Sales Days—he grew his company to $2.7 million with a 50% gross profit. The following year, his sales reached $3.4 million. He's now on track, three years later, to do $7 million.

When you refuse to accept mediocrity, everything changes.

The average year has 260 sales days, excluding weekends and holidays. Through our workshops and coaching, we've found that the typical salesperson experiences, on average, two mediocre sales days a week. This is unacceptable. A mediocre sales day is one where you've neglected your non-negotiable activities, failed to win the moments, or opted to not make that additional call. It's a day where you blew off training, tracking, and your fanatical approach to growth. If you don't sign a contract, but you still honored your high-level code of conduct and controlled what you had control over, that would count as a win for you that day.

Two mediocre days a week where you're not at your best can be costly. When multiplied by the number of salespeople you employ, the impact can be catastrophic.

Two days like this a week, over 50 weeks a year, amounts to 100 mediocre sales days. That's 38% of available sales days where you chose not to show up at your best.

If a salesperson has a goal of $2,000,000 per year, that breaks down to around $7,700 per day needed. While I understand some industries have higher ticket prices and longer sales cycles, breaking it down to this level is eye-opening. Two mediocre days multiplied by 100 days equals $770,000 in lost sales production. Every day we allow medioc-rity, we're pissing away $7,700.

For companies struggling to make ends meet, it's crucial to get fanatical about these days. Create your non-negotiable sales activities that will compound over time and bring the results you want. Remember how momentum works? This is what Anthony does. Every day is a sales day. Moving from $300k to $3.4 million, then to $7 million, was the result of this commitment.

For those who are selling, making some profit, and not lying awake at night wondering how you're going to make ends meet, I want you to look a few years into the future. What will the compound effect be of tolerating mediocrity in your sales team? How much will it affect the amount of money you're offered when you want to sell? How many millions will that stack up to be? Or, maybe you dream of step-ping aside and hiring someone to run the company as you move to a founder role. Every mediocre sales day you tolerate pushes that back a few days.

Recently, I did this exercise with a business owner running a $20 million company. She employs five salespeople and was shocked to see the compounding cost of mediocre sales days in her business annually. She shared, "I know they're not bringing their best. They're good people, but we've never done anything to give them a map of how to succeed more."

I replied, "This is a simple fix. It will require setting a new expecta-tion of winning and living it out as an example. It won't be easy, and you'll probably get some pushback. But there's a straightforward solution."

As leaders, we must set and honor the new code of conduct. We need to show integrity in our words and actions. It's futile to tell the team that mediocrity is unacceptable without providing consistent support and measurement. I recommend starting with owning your part in this. Get real and share how your lack of attention in this area is hurting everyone. Remember, when they see what's in it for them (WIIFT), they will pay attention.

> *"What kind of organization would you have*
> *if you created a supportive culture where*
> *mediocrity was despised by all?"*

Where are you allowing mediocrity to show up in your sales game? Remember, sales are the result of implementing a few controllable tasks each day. What is in your control right now that is getting your scraps? Is it prospecting? Follow up? Training? Identify it, create a plan, and honor the plan without compromise.

Annihilating mediocrity starts with an outright hatred for losing. I hate losing. In fact, I hate losing more than I love winning. I hate losing more when I know I didn't consistently win the moments I had control over. To me, that is failure. If I do my part and don't get the result, then I call it a lesson.

To win consistently at high levels, you must stop beating yourself. Take professional sports as an example. When most head coaches are interviewed and asked about the keys to winning the game, almost 100% of the time, they will mention eliminating mental mistakes, protecting the ball, or limiting penalties. They emphasize this because they recognize that every team has talented players. If talent alone were the key to winning, then everyone would win. Similarly, in your business, you compete with other talented companies daily. By limiting your "friendly fire" and consistently controlling the things you can, you will find yourself winning more often.

My hatred for losing is the fire in my gut—it keeps me sharp, hungry, and dangerous. You better find yours… or get used to getting your ass kicked. It could be your disgust for losing, your love for the process, a dream for your family, or maybe even how you want to stick it to your old boss or prove your dad wrong. Find the fuel that will be the foundation for your commitment to "No Mediocre Sales Days." There's too much at stake to half-ass this.

Everything we do and everything we don't do matters. Unleashing the sales success you want always comes back to personal discipline. This is your edge. Eliminate the mediocre sales days, and everything else in your organization will be easier.

You might be thinking, *I'm in! I get it! I just don't know where to start.* So let's dig in and give you a plan.

First, get clear on what's needed. Without clarity, you'll be unfocused and inconsistent. Get clear on your break-even revenue goal. This is the amount you need to deposit into the bank each year to "break even." This point is where all income and expenses balance out —you've paid for everything you needed without losing or making money. If you don't own a business and are working as a salesperson, figure out the amount you need to bring in that covers all of your goals.

Next, set your net profit goal. I personally think in terms of dollars, not percentages. Net profit is the financial reward you get for running the business well. You deserve to make money; otherwise, working for someone else might be a better option.

Here's an example of how this might play out: Suppose your annual break-even revenue is $500,000, found by dividing your overhead by your actual gross profit percentage.

Overhead / Actual Gross Profit = $500,000

Next, you set a net profit goal of $200,000.
Now, divide your break-even revenue by the number of sales days in the year—let's use 260:

$500,000 / 260 = $1,923.00

This is what you need to sell each day on average to break even. Do the same with the $200,000 of net profit, which amounts to $769 per day.

$200,000 / 260 = $769

Add them together, and you get $2,692.

$1,923 + $769 = $2,692

(Round it up to $2,700), and you now have your daily target to cover bills and hit your profit goal. You now have a clear target to pursue.

To calculate your own daily sales target, I've created a worksheet and more video examples for you to follow.

It's part of the bonus book resources you'll find here:

Next, calculate the number of leads you need to hit that target based on your average ticket size and sales closing rate.

The second part of this two-part plan is to establish a few daily non-negotiables that will generate those leads. It might be making 100 cold calls a day, visiting a certain number of existing clients, or sending [X] number of emails to your database.

This is in addition to all the other marketing your company is doing. The key is to create daily and controllable non-negotiables that lead to generating sales opportunities. In The Contractor Fight, one of my personal daily non-negotiables is sending five individual and personalized messages a day to our clients. This strategy moves the needle, as I'll discuss in more detail in Chapter 13.

Once you've determined your daily non-negotiables, you need to execute them. I am aware that there are many demands on you. However, if you did this correctly, you would have clarity over the exact activities you control that consistently lead to sales. Clarity of your target and consistency of controllable actions are key to eliminating mediocre sales days.

CHAPTER 5
THE STORIES WE FEED OURSELVES

You are what you eat: junk in, junk out; good in, good out. The same goes for our minds.

What you believe about yourself will be the result of the stories you tell yourself. I grew up hearing, "Rebers don't make money." Making money was for other people, the ones who lived on the other side of town. The specific environment we grow up in sets the tone for our thoughts. Repeatedly hearing things like "It's hard to make money" or "Wealthy people are assholes," I soon adopted these beliefs—and my bank account reflected them.

The average person has about 60,000 thoughts per day, with approximately 90% of these being negative if left unchecked.[1] Most of these thoughts are subconscious and operate on autopilot. The seeds of these thoughts are planted throughout our lives, and unfortunately, human beings tend to give them a negative slant.

As salespeople, we carry these thoughts into how we show up each day. When I was in grade school, I spent a couple of years in a Special Education class. I actually rode the 'short bus' to school and spent my days away from the life I had known in the previous years of school.

1. Chipman, P.R., 2014. *Overcoming the five primary negative thoughts: A twenty-one day mind renewal plan for men.* Liberty University.

As I grew older, it became more difficult for me to engage with anything that happened in school. I struggled to pass classes and to find interest in anything being taught. The only reason I graduated high school was my love for football, which kept me eligible. Football was the one thing that led me to graduation day.

After high school, I did everything I could to dodge anything that smelled like an intellectual challenge. I tapped out of college after one lame-ass semester and ran straight into the Marine Corps. Even there, I half-assed any shot at leveling up mentally—barely read, barely studied, and definitely didn't push myself. I kept my mouth shut around people I cared about, afraid they'd figure out I wasn't as smart as I wanted to be. And when I looked at careers after the Corps, I didn't ask what lit me up—I asked, *"Does this mean more school?"* If the answer was yes, I was out.

Later on, in a business partnership, I made a habit of biting my tongue and stuffing down what I really thought about how things should run. And on the rare occasion I did speak up, I folded the second someone pushed back. I didn't trust my gut. I didn't trust my instincts—even though time proved I was right more often than not. But instead of standing my ground, I played small… and paid for it.

I could continue with examples of how I was choosing to show up in the world: insecure about my intellectual abilities. The root issue was that I thought I was stupid. I rode the short bus. I was in Special Ed. I scored a 15 on the ACT. I struggled in school compared to the other kids who were 'smart.' I told myself I was stupid. This was the story I was feeding myself: junk in, junk out.

> *"I thought I was stupid, so I took actions—*
> *or inactions—that confirmed my beliefs."*

I didn't study. I didn't read. I didn't ask for help. I settled for my lot in life as a "stupid" person. I avoided intellectual confrontation and caved almost immediately when required to negotiate or debate anything.

My actions were the result of my thoughts.

One night, when I was about 24 years old, I had a beer with a friend. I was making $14 an hour painting houses. He was earning a base salary of $45,000 plus commission as a sales rep for a large company. His total compensation was over $100k.

I came home each night tired and dirty and just marginally better than broke. He came home each night a little wealthier.

"You should get into sales," he said casually between sips of his beer.

"I'm not sure I could do that type of a job," I replied, then quickly changed the subject.

What I really meant was, "That sounds intimidating to me. It sounds like a 'smart' person's job. I'd have to learn about a product and how to communicate that information to people who were way smarter than me." Instead of trusting myself to embrace the challenge and level up my skills, I chose to believe the negative self-talk and stories I had told myself on autopilot for so long.

A number of years later, I learned that we become what we think. Our thoughts lead to the results we get in life. In other words, we get more of what we focus on. If I tell myself, consciously or unconsciously, that I'm dumb, I will see more of that in my life. If I change the story and intentionally tell myself that I'm capable of learning new things and experiencing more success, I will see more of that in my life.

I created an acronym to remind myself of the power of being intentional with the stories I tell myself so I don't unintentionally hijack my success.

T-BAR: *Thoughts, Beliefs, Actions, Results.*

Somewhere along the line, I began changing the thoughts I put into my head. Instead of telling myself, "I'm not good at learning things like this," I started adopting new narratives like, "I am capable of learning this just like thousands of other people have." I learned to reframe my negative self-talk.

I started experimenting with affirmations. You've heard of them, right? Some call them "I am" statements. Our lives are the result of the stories we tell ourselves. The thoughts we inject into our minds are crucial to who we become and what we achieve.

Here's a crash course on what I believe about T-BAR: Our thoughts

—what we tell ourselves—become our beliefs. We act, or don't act, based on what we believe. Our actions earn us our results. Simple.

As I mentioned earlier, most of the tens of thousands of thoughts we think each day are subconscious. They're on autopilot, and many are negative. We are constantly undermining ourselves with the barrage of thoughts we allow to float around our heads:

- *I'm stupid.*
- *Making money is hard.*
- *My wife doesn't like me.*
- *Prospecting doesn't work.*
- *Prospects are all cheap.*
- *Nobody will pay our prices.*
- *I don't have time for _____.*
- *I'm not good enough to do that.*
- *I'm not important.*
- *People in my family have always been fat/broke/unhappy.*

Tell yourself something enough times, consciously or subconsciously, and you'll believe it.

> *"Our minds, left unchecked, are a terrible propaganda machine working overtime to derail our success."*

Be intentional about what you put into your mind. Do all you can to control your thoughts because they become your beliefs. You will act in accordance with what you believe. For example, if you tell yourself (thought) that prospecting doesn't work or is a waste of time, you will soon believe it to be true (belief). Your mind will seek evidence to prove you right. This belief will prevent you from picking up the phone, knocking on doors, and building new relationships (action), which, in turn, will mean you do not consistently crush your sales targets and earn more money (result). Friendly fire in full force.

You're telling yourself a story. Is it beneficial to you? If not, choose to reframe and rewire your thoughts.

People just aren't buying right now, becomes *I know many are fearful to commit to a purchase like this, but I only need a couple. I know there are a few in this city of 500,000 people, and I look forward to connecting with them.*

I don't have time becomes something like: *I have a lot on my plate right now, but I can figure out a way to give 30 minutes a day to level up my skills and train.*

What we think becomes what we believe. We act in accordance with our beliefs and get the results those actions produce.

Winning in sales requires taking the right actions. It means choosing the most appropriate action for the situation in front of you.

Be intentional about what you feed your mind. Tell yourself the right stories. Develop self-awareness about your thoughts and train yourself to correct them on the fly.

Your brain has a bundle of nerves called the Reticular Activating System (RAS). Its job is essentially to filter out unimportant things and help you find more of what you tell it is important. This is why our self-talk is so crucial. Your brain works overtime to prove you right.

Read that again: ***"Your brain works overtime to prove you right."***

Allowing negative narratives only encourages your brain to find more evidence to support them.

I believe one reason many people don't achieve what they want is that they spend more time focused on their current situation or problems than on the things they desire. Examine your thoughts. Ensure they align with what you want more of, and then get ready for more of that to show up!

Selling Unafraid requires the self-awareness and discipline to be intentional about your thoughts. I've seen countless salespeople struggle simply because they lack the discipline to reframe their circumstances, focus on what they want more of, and do the work required.

CHAPTER 6

CONQUER THE CIRCUMSTANCES

During the Great Recession, our painting company revenue took a beating. The phones were quiet. People held onto their money tightly, and everything in business was harder.

The years prior to that season, money was flowing. We used to joke that as long as you didn't kick someone's pet or throw up in their home, you would walk out of 90% of sales appointments with a deposit check and a new client.

Many salespeople become nothing more than order-takers when times are good. We grow complacent and expect things to be easy. They are easy until they are not, and that's what 2007–2009 brought.

Throughout our lives, the field conditions will change. The economy does what it does. Regulations are implemented that disrupt the business plan that had been working for many years. One of your kids gets diagnosed with autism. You get divorced. Your company hires a new CEO who makes changes to your product.

Looking back over your life, how many times have the conditions changed? Sometimes, we drive the change intentionally; sometimes, it's caused by our own friendly fire and mistakes. And other times, it just is what it is, without any wrongdoing on our part.

HOW CAN THIS BECOME THE BEST THING THAT HAS EVER HAPPENED?

When our phones went silent and our business entered new circumstances, we had a choice. We could either complain about it and play the victim or choose to control what we could control. The field conditions were what they were, and success didn't care. Success requires us to do what is required regardless of how we feel about it or what new field conditions present themselves.

We chose to reframe the story. While the majority were living in fear and allowing themselves to be consumed by worry, we chose to attack. I asked, "How can this end up being the best thing that's ever happened to our business?"

Speaker and entrepreneur Ed Mylett would say, "This is happening for you, not to you."

We rallied the troops. We created a new budget. Cut owner pay by 30% and everyone else's by 20%. We slashed anything in our overhead that wasn't making or saving us money. We had a company meeting and told the truth to everyone. I shared how I believed we were stronger together than apart but understood that they needed to do what they needed to do for their families. I created a performance plan that would put more money in their pockets when targets were hit. I learned how to build the brand and generate leads without having a lot of money to do it.

These things were in our control.

We also reached out to and gave fanatical attention to our past clients and increased our prospecting activities.

These things were also in our control.

I want to stress that there were many emotions in the room the day we "rallied the troops." My partner and I were embarrassed that we hadn't made some moves sooner. We were terrified that all of them would bail, and we'd be left staring at each other at the end of the meeting. Reframing the story started with a decision, accomplished by working through the negative emotions and self-talk that can so easily keep us from doing what is required.

Far too often, when faced with challenging circumstances, we get stuck. We stop moving. We stop dreaming. We block out any optimism and allow the self-talk to take over. This is what the mediocre sales-person does. The elite show up and honor the code, no matter what comes their way.

Winners find a way to win. Losers use adversity as an excuse.

Looking back on the Great Recession, it ended up being the best thing that ever happened to me as a business leader. I learned to be a better leader. It forced me to communicate at deeper levels and pushed me to learn how to truly unify our team, living out the saying, "We have each other's backs." I became a better marketer. These new field conditions drove me to get more creative and delve into using social media and content creation to attract our ideal clients. The recession improved my sales skills because, more than ever, competitors were slashing prices and working for free. We raised our prices, and even though our revenue took a beating, our profit increased.

The conditions you face each day are yours, and they're real. You may be weighed down and overwhelmed. Maybe you're paralyzed by new conditions and at a loss about what step to take next.

Choose to conquer the new field conditions. This starts with acknowledging them: "I see you."

Then, commit to finding a workaround and start asking yourself better questions. Instead of "This economy is killing our sales. Nobody wants to buy. How can I sell more?" ask, "If this were the forever normal, what would differentiate us and cause us to be a magnet for our ideal clients?"

Anthony Robbins puts it this way, "Successful people ask better questions, and as a result, they get better answers."

I have taken that quote to heart over my career. Ask better questions. Get better answers to conquer the new circumstances.

After you've acknowledged the circumstances and committed to finding solutions, it's time to attack. Execution is where most drop the ball.

Bring your best to the implementation of your plan. Your best is controllable; it's in nobody's hands but yours. I believe when you commit to bringing your best to whatever circumstances you face, you will always find a way to win.

It might take some time. The results will most likely lag behind the work. Remember, time will pass anyway. The conditions may or may not change. How will you wish you had shown up after a month goes by? How would you be better if, after a year or two of tough circumstances, you had built the habit of choosing to reframe and bring your best to each moment?

As I write this, inflation is at an all-time high. Fear is everywhere. The 'experts' say things will probably get a lot worse. I just received a text from a client saying things are getting harder and how he's looking to sell some equipment and figure out how to run a leaner company.

New circumstances.

A new normal for a while.

I constantly remind our clients to choose to acknowledge the facts and then to focus on what they can control. Ignoring the truth won't help anything. Neither will sitting back and waiting for it to pass. I reminded the client who texted me to honor the code he set for himself and his company. I reminded him that success is usually inconvenient and to keep showing up. Winners find a way to win.

How important is it for you to succeed? Get clear on what success looks like in your sales role and understand the implications if you don't succeed.

Do you feel a desire to succeed as much as you want to breathe? If not, you're probably not fully aware of the implications, or you might be aiming at the wrong targets. Your goals should weigh on you. I believe the pressure to win is beneficial. It's where we grow. It's how we recognize that our goals are significant and deserving of our best effort every day.

> *"When you view your success as necessary, as crucial,*
> *as non-negotiable, the conditions won't matter.*
> *You will find a way to win."*

The mediocre person looks for reasons to give up. They eagerly await the next excuse to present itself. Challenging circumstances are an opportunity to prove yourself, as shared by the Roman Stoic philosopher Seneca a few thousand years ago:

"No man is more unhappy than he who never faces adversity.
For he is not permitted to prove himself."
–Seneca

Elite salespeople love to compete. They relish the opportunity to test themselves. Difficult challenges reveal our true character, and the elite embrace them.

Instead of saying, "Oh, no!" they exclaim, "Hell yeah! Bring it on!"

If the field conditions are becoming more difficult for you, it's time to connect with why your success is necessary. When you can feel this necessity in your DNA, you will flip the bird to whatever circumstances attempt to hijack you.

Find a way to win.

PART 2
CONNECT

CHAPTER 7
MAKE ME FEEL IMPORTANT

My wife Lee and I were excited to plan our wedding in early 2022. We aimed to get married in August of 2022, which we did on the 20th. However, the venue we eventually decided on was not our first choice.

We live in Colorado Springs, surrounded by the badass beauty of Pikes Peak and the Front Range. When we pictured our wedding, we knew it had to be at a high-end resort with a killer view of the Garden of the Gods. We wanted that sunset hitting those massive red rocks—sandstone, limestone, all of it glowing like fire—as we said our vows. The raw, towering rock formations of the Garden of the Gods... there was no better place to lock it down with my soulmate.

We scheduled an appointment with the resort's wedding planner, looking forward to mapping out the perfect event. We were ready to sign the contract, drop a deposit, and mark it on the calendar. That was until we met the wedding planner, whom I'll call "Katie." I don't remember her real name because she gave me no good reason to do so.

We walked in and introduced ourselves. The moment we sat down, she pulled out the pricing sheets and began explaining the different packages and their respective price tags.

"Which one do you want to do?"

The Queen and I looked at each other in disbelief. We both knew the other was thinking, *WTF?* We were both pissed and frustrated. Her arrogance was off-putting. She approached the sale as if it were already a done deal.

Sales is about connection. The best, the elite, are masters at connecting with their prospects and understanding their goals and dreams. Connection starts with a simple concept I first heard from my good friend and one of our sales coaches, Derek Johnson. Derek excels at making others feel important, because they are, and his bank account reflects that. His coaching around this concept has changed the financial futures of thousands of families. Embracing this concept has the power to immediately increase sales and profit without special scripts or sales magic.

The concept?

Make me feel important.

This is a concept at which most salespeople fail. The energy they bring often feels like an annoyance, like they're thinking, *I don't want to be bothered.* Most salespeople, especially those who don't *SELL UNAFRAID*, are only thinking about themselves and closing the deal. How many times have you walked into a retail store and seen salespeople leaning against the counter, phone in hand, who finally look up and say, "Welcome in"?

What would it have looked like for Katie to make us feel important?

Let's start with gratitude. This is a key element that creates a strong connection with another human being. Your prospects have options, and for whatever reason, they choose to walk into your office or call your company to inquire about working with you. Gratitude is a secret weapon in sales. Lack of gratitude stems from a lack of perspective and understanding of reality. When I ran our painting company outside of Chicago many years ago, there were over 400 painting companies competing for business. Stepping back and considering what it meant for someone to pick up the phone and contact us was a game-changer. They chose us to talk to out of 399 other options. That demands gratitude.

Showing up with gratitude starts with a smile. Whether on the phone or in person, light up your face with a smile. Bring that energy to the first interaction they have with your company and watch your sales grow. When I teach our clients how to sell, I urge them to start with something like, "Joe, before we talk about your situation, I wanted to say thank you. I'm not sure what prompted you to contact us, but thank you. I know you have numerous options. Regardless of the outcome of our time together, I just want you to know I appreciate it."

How exceptional is that? What impact would it have on building rapport and moving closer to a deeper connection with a salesperson if they started with "thank you"?

The next component of connection is to choose to "be where your feet are." In other words, be fully present in this moment with this person. Steven Shinholser, my good friend and one of my business partners, would only conduct his sales calls from what he called "Command Central." It was his desk, surrounded by notes on the wall or Post-it notes stuck to his computer screen, reminding him to bring his best to the human being on the other end of the line. He wasn't in a loud coffee shop or driving; he was never distracted from being fully engaged with the person to whom he was speaking.

We've all experienced conversations where it's obvious the other person is "somewhere else." This communicates, "You're not impor-tant." You're not important enough for me to give my full attention to. Again, more friendly fire!

Consider how detrimental it is for a salesperson not to be 100% present. This is where they get paid! You spend time and money gener-ating sales opportunities. You're role-playing and training to get better. Then, when it's time to do what you've been training for, you show up with only a half-assed focus. It's inexcusable.

The words we speak are also crucial to the connection we make, determining how valued someone feels. The mediocre salesperson immediately presents the packages and lists all the reasons why they think they're the best choice. The mediocre salesperson focuses on their presentation, making it all about them, trying to prove why they're different or better than the competitors. That's what Katie did.

Not once did she ask a question about us. True connection happens when we uncover their reasons for wanting to buy and not focusing on all the reasons we think they should buy from us.

"People buy for their reasons, not ours."

This is where the next piece of the connection puzzle comes into play: Curiosity.

Genuine curiosity will launch your sales results to new levels. Instead of showing up to a call with an agenda, come with a clean slate and get to know them: their goals, their fears, and what would cause them to feel great about working with you.

Had Katie started with, "Tell me about your wedding day. Wave a magic wand and paint a picture for me," she would've heard twenty minutes of Lee and me sharing what we envisioned. We would've talked about the view at sunset, the time with our family and friends, the picturesque wedding day, and the party to follow. We would've spent another 30 minutes walking around the space, dreaming and selling it to ourselves. The meeting would've ended with a deposit check without Katie needing to do a damn thing. Instead, we left Katie's resort and never went back. We *settled* for another venue and gave them our $50k – far less than we would have been willing to pay for our dream.

Make me feel important.

Will your actions confirm what you say to your prospects and clients?

"We're grateful for you." Show me.

"You get our undivided attention." Then give it to me.

"We bend over backward for our clients." Prove it.

They came to you. The least you can do is make them feel important.

I'll close this chapter with a story my friend Aaron Harshaw shared with me about what happens when you are genuinely interested in the other person:

Leanne is a single mom who owns a two-story home.

As we discussed her desire for an updated bathroom, I sensed there was something more.

"What else is important to you?" I asked.

"Well, nothing in the bathroom," she said.

"Hmm, is there something important…elsewhere?" I probed gently—
then I shut the f*ck up.

"If I could have my dream," she started, then paused, as if to convey
that it could never happen.

"Ooh, a dream ask? Go on," I encouraged, with a hint of excitement in
my voice.

"If I could have my dream, I'd love to have a second laundry room on
the second floor," she said wistfully.

"A… second… laundry… room," I repeated slowly, letting the words
paint the picture. "That's super exciting. Tell me more."

"Well, the current laundry is in the basement, and our two bedrooms
are on the second floor. If I had my dream, it would be to have a desig-
nated laundry room on this floor. It would totally change my daily
life."

"Change your life? How so?" I asked.

Leanne went on for four or five minutes.

"Leanne, I have good news and bad news. Which would you care to
hear first?" I inquired.

"The good news, I guess," she said reluctantly.

"The good news is that together, we can design a space to change your
daily life with a second laundry on the second floor," I said with a big
smile.

"You can?!"

"We can!"

"What's the bad news?" she asked.

"The bad news is, doing so won't be cheap." I again STFU.

"I don't care. I want a new bathroom and a laundry room upstairs."

We sold that project last week.

CHAPTER 8
PEEL, DON'T POUNCE

There's a saying in the sales world: Show up and throw up.

That's the salesperson who vomits all their knowledge into their prospects' ears. They vomit their features. They vomit their benefits. They barf out all they know from all their years of experience. They spew out information about their awards, what they think people should do to solve their problems, and anything else they think will help them impress the prospect and close the deal.

Tim Cutroni is another one of our sales coaches and also an extremely successful and profitable contractor, and he is a master of connecting with prospects and helping them discover on their own whether he's a good fit for them. Many years ago, when Tim was a member in our program, he shared an insight he achieved after several months of exceptional sales success.

> *"Guys, the dumber I am,*
> *the more money I make."*

When Tim mastered what we're discussing in this section, it changed not only his life but also the lives of his wife Janelle, their kids, and ten grandkids! Tim is a master of what I call "Peel, Don't Pounce."

Before I grasped this concept, I would pounce on any sign that showed the prospect we were qualified to work for them. If they mentioned, "We're really embarrassed by how the house looks. The colors are outdated and need a refresh," I would immediately respond with something like, "We paint hundreds of homes a year and offer color consultations. We can help you pick the right colors and bring your house up to date with current trends."

Pounce! Look at me! I'm amazing!

People buy for one of two reasons: pain or pleasure. Most salespeople know this but don't always know how to use that knowledge effectively. So, they pounce, trying to impress.

When I began to understand this, it forever changed the way I sold.

I knocked on Scott's door at the scheduled time, eager to talk about painting his house. After exchanging pleasantries in the foyer, I asked, "Tell me why I'm here today."

Scott explained that they had never been happy with the paint job the last company did a couple of years earlier. He mentioned the quality was lacking and regretted hiring them.

The old Tom would have pounced, assuming that the most important thing to Scott was quality. "We paint hundreds of homes and have amazing reviews. We always produce work to the highest standards, which is why we have so much repeat business." *Barf!*

However, as you'll see in a moment, quality, though important, was not Scott's top priority.

Instead, I responded by peeling back what he shared with a question. Then another. And another. Until I was at the root of what we call "The Motive"—his reasons for buying.

"Scott, it sounds like that was a frustrating experience. What would've made it a great one?"

"I could've lived with some of the quality issues, but what really pissed me off was how they left the house each night. I travel a lot and was gone the week they were here. Every night, when I would call home to talk to the family, my wife gave me the third degree about the painters. She was ticked they left tools lying around. She had to clean up after them every day. She was mad at me for hiring them. She was worried one of the kids would step on a tool and hurt themselves."

Pouncing would sound like, "We never leave a mess, and we Swiffer the floors at the end of every day, blah, blah, blah."

I chose to, as Tim calls it, play dumb.

"You caught grief for that every night?" *Peel.*

The essence of peeling, or playing dumb, is curiosity. When you're curious, you ask questions and avoid making assumptions about what's important to someone. Being curious communicates that what they're saying is important—that they are important.

With each question, delivered with the appropriate tone and spirit of the conversation, Scott grew increasingly frustrated recalling that experience. His wife had to babysit a crew of grown men along with her own kids. She was pissed!

After a few rounds of this, still standing in the foyer, I asked the question that unearthed the root of his pain and positioned us as the only obvious choice for their next project.

"I'm sorry to hear all that. I imagine it really tested your patience. But, I'm curious… when you came home from your trip, what was the vibe like in the house?"

Scott's face reddened. A vein popped out on his neck as he said, "She was so mad at me she made me sleep on the couch for two nights." I'm sparing you the colorful language he used.

Before I share how I brought the sale home, I want to highlight a couple of things. First, Scott felt heard. I made him feel important. I did the opposite of what all the other salespeople had done—simply walk around, measure, and spit out a price. Second, this conversation might seem intrusive to some, but the spirit was collaborative and open. The conversation made Scott and me allies in ensuring this never happened again. Finally, I got to the root of his pain. He didn't want to put his wife through anything like that again. He was embarrassed for making the choice he made last time and wanted to get it right this time.

"Scott, before I do my thing here, what would need to happen for you and your wife to feel you had the best experience you could ever have with a painting company?"

He thought for a moment and replied, "I don't want my wife to clean up after anyone."

"That's fair. I have a crazy idea. What would happen if I wrote it into the contract that if your wife had to spend one second of her life cleaning up after our crew, the entire project would be free?"

"You'd do that?" he asked.

"I would," I replied.

"The job is yours."

"I haven't even told you how much it's going to be. Most homes like yours are in the $20,000–$30,000 range."

"That's fine. I know you're our guy."

Contract signed. Deposit check collected. New project on the calendar.

This is the power of the peel. Slow down. Breathe. Ask an open-ended question and shut your mouth. When they answer, repeat the process until you uncover their Motive. Then, and only then, are you truly ready to discuss money. It's a major mistake to rush to discuss the money without first establishing the foundation and connection that occurs in The Motive phase. (We discuss money in the second step of the sales process we teach.)

All of your awards, experience, and knowledge are important, and there's a time for all that—if it's important to the prospect. If not, there's no need to mention it. As you ask questions and peel back the layers, what is important to them will become clear.

Remember Katie? The wedding planner we didn't hire? Imagine if she had taken the time to peel.

"Lee, can you share with me what you want to feel when you walk down the aisle, with all your family and friends there and Tom waiting for you? Paint that picture for me. I know this is important to you, and I want to get this right."

No matter what you sell, the *peel* is always better than the *pounce*.

CHAPTER 9
HOW TO GET THE MOTIVE

In the last chapter, I touched on "The Motive." Our sales training process, called Shin-Fu, includes five steps, with The Motive being the first. Because The Motive is the most important step and the one that will lead to deeper connections, which in turn sets the table for the rest of the sale, I thought it made sense to devote a chapter to it.

Shin-Fu is named after my former partner and co-founder of our sales training program, Steve Shinholser (whom you met previously). Many years ago, a coaching client said to Steve, "The way you navigate sales calls is amazing, and the way you handle objections—it's like some kind of sales kung fu. It's Shin-Fu!" Fast-forward ten years, and we've trained thousands of men and women in the art of Shin-Fu.

The five-step process looks like this:

1. **The Motive**: Dig into the "why" behind the project using questions and listening actively.
2. **The Money**: Use bracketing to ensure you're on the same page as the prospect about the budget.
3. **The Truth**: Set the expectation that you will be honest with each other and will agree to move forward or not, without excuses.

4. **The Influencers**: Make sure all necessary players are on board.
5. **The BS Meter**: Use a consultation fee to separate the liars from the buyers.

Each step involves more complexity than described above and is mastered through consistent role-play training.

In most cases, The Motive occurs during the initial pre-qualification call, before spending hours meeting with prospects. Most salespeople could reclaim 50% of their sales time if they were properly pre-qualified using Shin-Fu.

The 5 Steps of the Shin-Fu Sales Process are included with your bonus resources available as part of your book purchase

Scan the QR code:

Of course, in-person meetings are necessary throughout the sales process; just ensure you're spending time with prospects who are a good fit.

A Shin-Fu call can be conducted in a 15–20 minute phone call or even a Zoom video call before any in-person meetings.

This pre-qualification call is like the pre-date. If you've been on a dating app, you swipe around until someone catches your eye. Then, a direct message is sent. There's some back and forth about each other until you both decide if it makes sense to go on a date.

The Motive is all about determining if we can even help you with your situation. Before we set up a time to meet, let's have an open and honest conversation about whether or not I can help you and establish the ground rules. If so, let's go on a date. If not, we can part ways, and nobody has wasted their time.

I believe there are four keys to uncovering the true Motive of your prospect:

1. Ask open-ended questions that get them talking.
2. Listen with curiosity and peel back layers.
3. Summarize what was shared to show you understand them.
4. Embrace silence—or, as we like to say, STFU.

ASKING OPEN-ENDED QUESTIONS

The power of the questions you ask is immense. People buy for one of two reasons: pain or pleasure.

Some examples of pain include:

- Embarrassment about how ugly their yard is, which in turn keeps them from entertaining.
- Running a great restaurant with amazing food, but nobody knows it exists, so sales are low.
- They have a roof that is leaking and is destroying their belongings, costing them thousands of dollars to replace, along with other repairs needed as a result of the leak.

Pleasure might look like this:

- Building your dream house in Santa Fe, New Mexico with amazing mountain views.
- Creating a kitchen that brings the family together for more positive memories.
- Planning the dream wedding with picturesque sunset views of the Garden of the Gods.

Your job is to guide the prospect to the best solution for them. Open-ended questions will help you achieve this. An open-ended question is one that cannot be answered with a "yes" or "no" or with short, direct responses. The purpose of the question is to get them talking about themselves!

Open-ended questions are crucial for several reasons. First, they often reveal something you wouldn't expect about the prospect or their reasons for buying. By asking these questions and peeling back their answers, they will describe what they want in more detail. Asking questions and peeling instead of pouncing also helps develop a deeper connection and trust between you and the prospect.

LISTEN WITH CURIOSITY

Most people listen with an agenda. We listen but don't truly hear them. To understand The Motive, listen with a curious mind. That means listening with the intent to understand, not just waiting for your turn to speak. When you listen with curiosity and with the intent to genuinely help, you'll hear things like, "I just feel like you get me, and we want to move forward with you."

Here's an example from one of our BATTLEGROUND members about the power of The Motive. BATTLEGROUND is our group coaching program that helps home improvement contractors build stronger and more profitable businesses.

My first big renovation project, and biggest sale to date, was with a divorcee who moved to a new town and purchased a half-plex. She loved the location and the size because she wanted to force herself to get rid of 80% of her stuff. She had her niece telling her that she knew other contractors who could do the job for a lot less. I didn't want to lose this job, but I also knew I couldn't sell it for any less than we discussed. I met with her for what I thought was going to be the last time. We sat on a stone bench in front of another job I was working on, and she happened to be renting a house two doors down. I looked her in the eyes and asked, "How will you know which one of us is the better fit for you?"

She responded, "I know you are. You listen to me, and I trust you. I don't trust the other guy."

I asked, "What do you think we should do next?"

She said, "You mentioned something about paperwork."

We signed the contract for $200,000. A few weeks later, she made a design change. That design change added $25,000 to the project.

Total project price: $225,000.

– Al, Remodeling Contractor

Al built trust because of his ability to listen with curiosity. She felt heard and understood.

SUMMARIZE WHAT WAS SHARED TO SHOW YOU UNDERSTAND THEM

After the prospect shares their thoughts and desires with you, repeat it back to clarify you got it right. It might sound like this:

"Joe, from what I understand, your main concern is making sure the yard is completed by April 7th so you have time to complete some other things that need to be done before your daughter's graduation party in May. You also mentioned making sure that we don't use any loud machines between 2:00 and 3.30 p.m. each day because your son naps at that time. Did I get that right?"

This ensures that you understand them and strengthens their trust in you. By summarizing what they've shared, you once again prove that you understand what's most important to them.

SHUT THE F*CK UP

Most salespeople talk too much, likely because they haven't put in the reps required in training, so they fall back on what they're most confident in—talking about their industry knowledge! Silence is your ally. The majority of what comes out of your mouth should be open-ended questions and statements that encourage them to talk more. The more they talk, the better you will understand what's most important to them about who they choose to hire.

Silence can be uncomfortable if you're not accustomed to it. Our natural inclination is to fill the silence, so we talk. Don't make assumptions during those brief moments of silence. Often, the prospect is processing their thoughts. By breaking the silence, many salespeople talk themselves out of a deal or higher profits.

When I was still a knucklehead salesperson, I once told a prospect that the total for their project would be $15,000. After stating the price, I tried to let it linger in… silence. But due to my lack of training, I got impatient and said, "We could also discount the project by 10% if that helps."

He replied, "I was ready to go with it at $15k, but I'll take the $1,500 off. Thank you!"

In a world where profit is everything, I stole $1500 from myself and my business because I didn't STFU.

This was one of the many costly lessons I learned through the years. Now, silence and I are good friends.

You never know what someone is thinking, so don't try to be a mind reader. In a similar situation months later, with a $40,000 project on the line, I allowed the silence to stretch. It felt like an eternity, although it was only about 10 seconds. He finally broke the tension by saying, "Sorry. I'm good with this and ready to go. I'm just thinking about which account I want to move the money from."

Make no assumptions, and let silence work to your advantage.

There are hundreds of potential word tracks you can use to gather the information needed to determine if you and your prospect are a good fit. Below, I will share a few of my favorites with you.

Remember, these word tracks, used without the right spirit, tonality, and curiosity, aren't enough. They do nothing for you if you don't genuinely listen, peel back layers, and summarize to ensure you understand them.

"Lee, I'm excited to learn more about what's important to you on your wedding day. I want to see what you see. Would you mind painting me a picture of that?"

"How are you hoping I can help you?"

"If you could wave a magic wand over all this, what would it look like?"

"What would it look like if you had to live with this issue for another year or two?"

"So, you've gotten three estimates already? What are you hoping to hear from me that you haven't heard from the other three companies?"

"How will you know you've hired the right company?"

"What issues have you had with contractors in the past that you hope we don't repeat?"

"That's an interesting question; how do you mean?"

"If the experience with your painter were to work out perfectly, how would that look to you?"

"How long have you been thinking about doing this? Just out of curiosity, what's prompting you to take action now?"

"What is your experience in working with a [whatever your trade is]?"

"Hey Joe, quick question for you… when you say you're looking at a few bids, what's going to matter most in how you choose who to hire? Just want to make sure we're the right fit for what you actually care about."

Notice how these questions are all designed to get them talking. The magic happens when they're talking *and* you're listening. The magic is in the question you ask next to further peel back and discover what's most important to them. I've had numerous experiences where the first "pain" they shared wasn't the real pain uncovered later. Ask enough of the right questions and continue to peel it back, and you'll find the answers you're looking for.

This is simply a conversation with another human being. You're uncovering the true motive. When that happens, a connection is made, and you differentiate yourself from your competitors. You become exceptional.

Here's another example of what happens when this is done properly. Here's Kelly's story:

How did we go from a $45k–$30k ballpark to a signed contract of $65k?
The answer is: LISTEN.

Here's the story.

> *I had a referral come to me for a refresh in her two bathrooms. I went through the Shin-Fu with her and dug deep to hear what she was truly asking for.*

When we came to the price, she was comfortable with the range but mentioned she should probably ask for more quotes. "After all, you are the only one who has given me anything!"

Instead of asking a question, I just STFU because I could sense she was about to say more.

"I mean, I had a guy come out here, but he has not given me a quote yet. And... I did not really feel comfortable with him." STFU: there was more coming.

"Honestly, Kelly, you are a breath of fresh air! You actually treat me like a human being! So, how do we move forward with you and get this project started?"

Letter of Intent signed and deposit taken. BUT THAT'S NOT ALL!

Fast-forward to the onsite meeting, and I couldn't believe what happened! As we were arriving, a flooring estimator was leaving. We paid no mind and proceeded to measure the two bathrooms she wanted refreshed.

As we were wrapping up, she approached me and said, "Kelly, I'm not sure I'm comfortable with the way they suggested laying the new floor in the kitchen. I think he was just trying to save me money."

They were planning on laying down luxury vinyl on the already built-up floor and they were concerned about the transition being too high. They also wanted to have a mat under the door as you walk in, but the current floor won't allow that.

We confirmed that adding another layer to the floor was possible, but it would build it up further. I asked if she was okay with that. In the background, I saw her husband shaking his head no. Seeing her uncertainty, I turned to her husband and said, "I see you shaking your head. What would you like to see happen with this floor?" He expressed his desire to have it brought back down.

At the end of the meeting, my clients expressed their discomfort with the other company and asked us to provide a quote.

AND THERE'S MORE...
We encountered an issue with one of the I-Joists being improperly cut by a previous plumber and called a time-out to discuss it. We had a lengthy discussion about the appropriate fix and asked them what they would prefer to do. They ultimately decided to fix it now rather than postponing the issue.

There was another way we listened to them. My client kept eyeing tile for the kitchen and bathroom but felt compelled to choose vinyl due to budget concerns.

I discovered her biggest pain point: fear of overspending on this project. They had finally reached a place of financial security where they didn't have to worry about money, and she was concerned about depleting their savings.

Knowing she really wanted tile, we decided to investigate the price difference ourselves.

It wasn't significant in the grand scheme of things, so we added it as an upgrade option on the proposal so she could see for herself.

We just went from a two-bathroom refresh at a ballpark of $45k–$35k to a whole new kitchen floor and upgraded tile for 65k.

THIS is why it is so important to listen to your clients!

THE SHIN-FU WORKS...USE IT!

– Kelly, Designer/Remodeling Contractor

Kelly created an environment where the client felt important. She kept putting it back in the client's court through her questions and peeling it back. Trust was built. Her client felt heard and understood. She involved the client's husband and asked about what he wanted. This didn't just happen because she had some word tracks. Kelly has completed more than 175 training role-plays in the past several months. She trains. She tracks. She consistently works on her skills with fanatical discipline. *Be like Kelly!*

Remember the story I shared in the introduction about the guy we had out to look at my basement floor? He lost the sale because he failed to get my Motive. If he had asked anything like, "What are your plans for the space?" he would have uncovered a treasure chest of emotional gold.

Him: "Tell me about your plan for this space…"

Me: "I broadcast from this area to people all over the world. I have a large podcast, YouTube, and social media presence, and I need this to be a place I can show on camera. Right now, it's a stupid-looking basement. I'm turning this into our FightHQ. I'll have a pool table here with cool I-Beam-looking legs, a tequila bar over here with a black granite counter and copper on the front of it—kind of like the bar at Sierra, one of our favorite restaurants. In this area, I will have a huge screen and a seating area for when certain clients come to town for coaching. The floor is the foundation for all of this, and whatever finish we do needs to be on-brand."

One question is all that was needed to get me to open up about *my reasons* for doing the project.

After I shared all that, what would it have taken to get me on the schedule?

Him: "It sounds like this floor is setting the tone for everything else in here. Is there anything else I need to know?"

Me: "I think that's it."

Him: "I've got two different ways I can approach this. Are you cool if we talk about money?"

Me: "Yep."

Him: "The first option would be the 'X500 super cool finish.' That would be between eighteen and twenty K. The second is the more basic 'Y200 finish,' and that will be around ten to twelve K. Which of those conversations would you like to have?"

I'll stop with the examples. You get the point. He'd be walking out with a deposit check.

Find The Motive and everything else is easier.

CHAPTER 10
MASTERING OBJECTIONS WITH EMPATHY

Merriam-Webster calls an objection "a feeling or expression of disapproval." In plain English? It's the reason your prospect won't hand over their money. It's them saying "no" or "not yet." But here's the part most salespeople miss—the key word is *feeling*. Objections aren't just logical roadblocks; they're emotional. Once that finally clicked for me, everything changed. I stopped getting defensive, stopped trying to bulldoze through them—and started responding in a way that actually moved the sale forward.

Before I go any further, I want to clarify what this chapter is NOT. I am not handing you a script. I'm not providing a word track for every situation you will face. I am sharing proven concepts and frameworks that, when practiced, will enable you to bring your own voice, meet the real needs of your clients and sell more of your stuff. Your commitment to finding The Motive, peeling back layers, and connecting with curiosity will provide you with the words when needed.

There are a few common mistakes average salespeople make when handling objections, which I will share shortly. However, the first and most crucial mistake is attempting to address an objection—an emotional matter—with logic and intellect. People buy based on emotion first and then justify the decision with logic. We all do it. We desire the "thing," and then we rationalize why it makes sense.

Always keep this in mind whenever you encounter objections like, "Your price is too high" or "I need to talk to my spouse." Emotion drives the decision-making process every time.

Other mistakes salespeople make in this area include:

- Ignoring the objection, hoping it will disappear with a bit more charm, or changing the topic.
- Fighting to justify your position.
- Getting defensive about the objection.
- Arguing with them because of all the knowledge you have about their problem.

You may be right, and they may be way off base. You might present the most logical argument ever for why they should buy your product or service. Just remember, emotion drives the decision-making process.

To effectively handle any objection thrown your way, it makes sense to take a moment and understand where these objections originate from.

First, they arise from a lack of trust. Salespeople have a reputation for being pushy. Your prospects' guard is up almost from the moment they interact with you. They want to protect themselves, as we all do. Until trust is established, you can expect some resistance. It's up to you to get ahead of the objections through approaches like:

- *The Content on Your Website*: Create content that addresses common questions, what things cost, and typical problems with your products or industry. The Bible on this topic is *They Ask, You Answer* by my buddy Marcus Sheridan. I highly recommend grabbing a copy.
- *Honor the Commitments You Make*: I recently spoke with a prospect for our coaching group, BATTLEGROUND. She shared that they had spoken to one of our main competitors a couple of weeks prior and crossed them off the list because they didn't call back when they said they would. This was after she shared that there was a lack of connection on the first call, and she didn't feel like he "got her."

- *Lack of Connection*: Without the emotional connection I talked about in The Motive and other parts of this book, the prospect stays at arm's length and continues to see the salesperson as an adversary rather than an ally.

Every interaction a prospect has with your company either builds trust or erects a wall. Do your part to continually make the case that you are bringing value and giving them a reason to trust you every step of the way.

Before I hit you with some word tracks and killer questions to handle the objections you're going face, I need you dialed in on four non-negotiable keys to winning:

1. Prepare for the Most Common Objections:

This is why training your ass off matters. You don't rise to the occasion—you fall to the level of your training. Most sales teams out there are winging it, not role-playing, and leaving millions on the table. You want to win? Get obsessed with practice.

2. Grab Their Emotion First:

Sick of me saying this yet? Too bad. People buy on emotion, then justify with logic. If you're not slowing down to peel back layers, summarize what they're feeling, and connect with what's going on inside their head—you're not leading. You're just reacting.

3. Show Up with Empathy:

Empathy isn't weak—it's a power move. Put yourself in their shoes. What's got them nervous? What crap experiences are they dragging into this conversation? Slow down. Listen. Make it safe for them to tell you the real story.

4. Put It Back in Their Court:

> Objection comes up? Acknowledge it. Don't argue. Then, hit them with a question that puts the ball right back in their hands. This isn't about pressure—it's about letting them own their decision. Some of my best sales results came from simply shutting up and giving them space to talk themselves into a yes.

The question I lean on is, "What do you think we should do next?" This, or a variation, is one of my "go-to" moves.

"Wow! You're $3k higher than the other companies!"

"I've heard that before. What do you think we should do next?"

"I need to think about this for a while."

"I can appreciate that. I've found that making decisions often comes down to having the right information rather than taking time to think. What do you think we should do next to get you the information you need?"

This strategy is effective for several reasons:

- You're implying a partnership with the client by using "we."
- You avoid needing to justify why your company does things a certain way.
- You're putting the ball in their court.
- You're in control because you are guiding the conversation.
- You'll have an opportunity to find a better solution because they are the ones who will propose it!

Challenge: Just try it and then shut up. They will lead you with their answer 100% of the time!

Another favorite strategy is playing "Let's pretend."

"I don't have the time for this right now."

"That's understandable. But let's pretend you did have the time for this. Would you do it?"

When they say "yes":

"Great. Let's dig in and figure out how to find you some time."

Objection handling, when built on the back of emotional connection, will significantly improve your close rates, repeat business, and referrals.

As we wrap this up, I'm going to leave you with a few more examples of how to handle the most common objections you'll run into. But listen—this isn't some cookie-cutter script for you to parrot. It's a framework. A guide. Your job is simple: help them figure out if *you're* the right fit for what they need. Not twist their arm. Not manipulate. If it's not a good fit, have the guts to walk—but if it *is*, help them see it and close the damn deal.

Cost

"That's more than I want to spend."

"I get that. Nobody wants to spend more than they need to. How much were you hoping to spend?"

"Your pricing is much higher than the other companies we've spoken to."

"I hear that from time to time. Why do you think they're priced so low?"

Getting Other Quotes

"We're waiting to hear back from a couple of other contractors."

"That's understandable. What are you hoping to hear from them that you haven't heard from me?"

Decision Makers

"I will have to speak with my spouse about this."

"I get that. What do you think they're going to say?"

They Want to Wait

"I need to think about it first."

"Usually, when someone says they need to think about it, it means I missed something. What question have I not helped answer yet?" or "What makes you say that?"

Too Much Money

"Your price is too high."

"I hear that now and then. What makes you say that?"

Continue to work to position yourself as an ally, not an adversary, and you can expect to increase not only your wins but also the size of your average sale, repeat, and referral revenue.

PART 3
HUNT

CHAPTER 11
CARRY YOUR WATER

At 10:00 a.m. on December 31st, 2022, my ass hit the couch, ready to watch college football. I love football bowl season. The Queen and a couple of our daughters were spending a week in Scottsdale, Arizona, for one of the girls' ballet intensives. We chose to hang there and enjoy the last week of the year away from the snow in Colorado Springs.

While watching football, I got to work. From 10:00 a.m. until 9:00 p.m., I worked the DMs with sales prospects for our training programs. By 9:00 p.m., I had signed up nine new clients and was fired up. At 9:00, the Queen said, "That's enough, let's play some games." I shut it down for the year and enjoyed time with the family.

My perfect day. Football and bringing people into our life-changing program. Heaven.

What was really happening was I was running through the finish line of 2022. I played through to the last echo of the whistle. I firmly believe that, as leaders, we have the responsibility to set an example of the type of effort we want to see from those we lead.

I'm all for time off, and I take it when I feel I need it—or when my CEO, Neil Kristianson, shoves me out the door for a while.

I believe everyone on a team should carry their own water and pull their weight. Of course, there are times when we need to cover for one another, as many have for me at various times in life. Going through a health issue, a divorce, bankruptcy, or another major life event are a few examples. However, that should be the exception, not the norm.

I believe it's unacceptable to have a day without a sale. That includes holidays.

Yep, I'm wired differently.

One of the biggest pet peeves I have with salespeople is their mindset regarding hunting. Elite salespeople hunt daily. They're competitive and love the challenge. They're what many would call a rainmaker—someone who rains money. They manufacture sales out of what seems to be thin air when, in reality, the sales come as a result of their consistent and fanatical mindset about prospecting.

The mediocre salesperson is a rain barrel waiting to catch the water from the heavens. Waiting to be fed like a baby bird—mouths open, waiting for the company to hand them a lead. Waiting for the "Google Gods" to bless them. Waiting for the marketing company to do their job better. They wait, and the result is mediocrity. They're nothing more than an order taker.

If you're in sales and not hunting, you're fooling yourself. Every day, tens of thousands of salespeople are waiting. They wait for the company to hand them a lead. They wait for the client to "get back to them." They wait to talk about money. Overall, they don't understand the importance of "RIGHT NOW." Time Kills Deals. If you want to become irreplaceable as a salesperson, be a hunter. Find your own leads. Return the call NOW. Send the email a minute ago. Everyone wants to eat, but few are willing to hunt. As a salesperson, you are only as good as the results you generate today. What you sold yesterday is old news. What you think you will sell tomorrow is a pipe dream. You're only as good as your performance today. Hunt.

Every day you take a passive approach to The Hunt is a day someone takes food off your family's table.

I spoke to a group of successful entrepreneurs a few months ago and asked a question.

"By a show of hands, how many of you wished your salespeople would produce a damn lead for themselves now and then?"

The response was electric. All 100 attendees shot their hands up in the air. Not because they don't want Google to cause their phone to ring. Not because they're unwilling to invest tens of thousands of dollars or more per month with their marketing agency. They want to know if their sales team cares enough to carry their water.

"It would be nice if now and then I knew my salespeople gave enough of a shit to open their mouth and make an effort," replied one attendee when I asked the group why it bothered them so much. Several others weighed in and agreed.

A good leader appreciates the results of their salespeople. I appreciate it when our salespeople get a signed contract. They train hard, bring their skills to the table, and make sales that help our clients win and the company reach its goals. I appreciate that. But, in addition to that, I'm even more grateful when they also lift a finger to build their own pipeline. When they self-generate a lead, I pay them more commission!

There's a reason why elite salespeople are highly recruited in their industry: they have their own book of business. They've built the habit of building their own pipeline, strengthening relationships, and making it rain.

In 2025, it's easier than ever to prospect with all the tools we have at our fingertips. Let me use an example outside of the construction industry to make my point. Pretend you sell mattresses in one of the brightly lit, 4,000-square-foot storefronts in the strip mall. I see you waiting, baby bird! And yes, I'm going way out of the box with this example.

You have a phone and several social media accounts. How about going live when the store is empty and talking about the importance of sleep? Educate us on anything that can help make my sleep better and why I need to care. Become known as THE EXPERT in the sleep game. Your expertise is sleep; you just happen to sell mattresses. Do this daily for the next 90 days and watch your sales grow!

My good friends Alan and Jodi Decker, owners of Decker's Pondscapes in Pattersonville, New York, make hundreds of thousands of dollars a year doing just that. One night, they went to their local pizza joint and were chatting it up with the owner. The owners shared that they were slow on Sundays. Alan said, "You should use your phone and go live." After some discussion on how to approach his live streams, Alan and Jodi headed for home.

A couple of weeks later, they went back, and the owner shared how the past Sunday was the best they ever had because he went live. He chose to hunt.

The elite live with their eyes open and search for opportunities. They use social media, hand out a card while waiting in line, and dial the number on the truck when they see a possible company they don't yet know.

The majority of financial struggles I see in small businesses result from not embracing the hunter mentality as a way of life. There is money all around you. Go get it. No more waiting. No more being a baby bird.

CHAPTER 12

PROSPECTING SUCKS, DO IT ANYWAY

A sk most salespeople what they think about prospecting, and they will say they hate it. Can you blame them? It's the one activity that breeds more rejection than anything else. Defined, it's nothing more than identifying and contacting potential customers for your business. Prospects are potential customers. Prospecting is finding other people who are potentially future customers.

Prospecting for gold—or panning for gold—is as simple as it gets. You grab a pan, step into the river, scoop up a bunch of mud and junk, and start shaking. All the useless crap washes away, and if you did it right, you're left with a little nugget of gold in the pan. Sales prospecting's the same damn thing—sift through the noise, shake off the tire-kickers, and find the people who are serious.

Simple concept.

Prospecting for sales is similar. You reach out to prospective clients, sifting through those that are not a good fit for whatever reason, and occasionally, you find some gold in the form of someone who wants to do business with you.

Simple concept.

Here's the rub: most people don't have the resilience to keep sifting. It's a grind, having conversation after conversation and hearing "go away," and most people give up after a certain amount of rejection.

In 2006, I received a phone call from a sales rep from a well-known national paint brand. He was the new guy and called to introduce himself. At the time, we bought 99% of our paint from another well-known company.

"Hi. This is Ryan with [XYZ], and I wanted to introduce myself. I'll be your point of contact from now on."

"Hi Ryan. Nice to meet you. I appreciate it, but we buy from [ABC] and have since day one. In fact, my family is full of painters, and if I switched, there would be hell to pay," I joked.

We had a brief and cordial conversation, and we both moved on.

A couple of weeks later, he called and invited me to a contractor appreciation event. I declined.

The next week, he stopped at a job site and brought our guys coffee.

He once shared with me, "You don't know it yet, but one day, you're going to give me a shot."

Ryan was relentless. He embraced standing in the cold river, scooping up mud, and going home with nothing to show for it, except a sore back and sunburn.

"No."

"We're good, man, thanks."

"We have no need to change suppliers."

"No."

"No."

"Dude, I know you're doing your job, but you really don't need to call on me anymore. I'd even be happy to put in a good word with your boss so he knows you're trying."

Steve Martin, the comedian and actor, famously said when asked how to become a successful comedian, "Be so good they can't ignore you."

Want to be elite in sales?

"Be so visible they can't ignore you."

I ignored Ryan for almost two years until I couldn't.

I received a call on a Friday afternoon from one of my Crew Leaders. It was 4:00 p.m., and he needed a 2-ounce jar of a certain colored putty to finish a custom mantle we were working on. In fact, he only needed a pinch of the putty. We had run short. It was 100% our fault. Now, it became my main vendor's issue. I called the [ABC] supplier and talked to the manager from whom we bought thousands of gallons of paint.

"Can you please run some putty out to this job for me? I'm over an hour away, and my guy can't leave the site if we're going to finish on time."

"Sorry. We can't for an order that small and with this late notice," he replied.

"You're joking, right?" I replied, annoyed.

"I'm sorry. I can't."

I hung up, searched through the voicemails on my phone to find Ryan's number, and pressed the call button.

"Hey Tom! What's up?"

I began with, "Ryan, you were right. You are going to get a shot, but probably not the first order you were hoping for."

Ryan went on to tell me he'd make it happen and appreciated me thinking of him. How could I not? He made it impossible for me not to know who to call. Sift, sift… little flake of gold.

Ryan's grit, energy, and refusal to get off my radar made that call happen. The dude personally drove a $7 item to a job site, forty minutes away, on a Friday afternoon—just so we could keep a promise to a client. That one inconvenient, pain-in-the-ass move showed me I mattered. And that closed the deal.

From that moment on, Ryan got *all* our business—just like that.

When you're out prospecting—or, as I like to call it, *hunting*—there are a few conditions for success. The best part? Every single one of them is 100% in your control.

START

Stop talking yourself out of it. "I don't have time" is not a valid excuse. Start anyway. "People don't want to be bothered." Again, who cares?. Start anyway. "I don't get results." Neither did Ryan until he did. Start anyway.

Not sure what to say? So what. Start. Be a human. Bring positive energy to others in a world where that's lacking. Play the long game and trust that all your sifting and shaking will provide a return in due time.

Here are a couple of my go-to word tracks that have generated millions in sales for me over the years. Don't overthink it. Just open your mouth and get better as you go.

"I see you build beautiful homes. We happen to paint them, and I thought it might make sense for us to know each other."

Fill in your prospect and your industry. I would do this while driving: when I'd see another company vehicle, I'd just dial the number. For example, I saw a van drive by, and I didn't recognize the company, Princeton Builders.

"Hi. Are you the guy driving on Route 59 near Ogden Avenue right now?"

He laughed and said, "Yeah. That's me. I'm Doug."

"Doug, you build stuff, and I paint stuff, and we don't know each other."

That simple call led to almost $500,000 of work each year.

"But, Tom, what do I say after the initial words come out of my mouth?"

I don't know. How about being curious and making them feel heard? That's probably a great place to start!

The next approach that worked well for me and many others is, "I see you all over and imagine you have 'a guy' for this, but I wanted to introduce myself in case you ever get in a bind. It never hurts to have a strong bench or a plan B. Would it be crazy for us to have a conversation?"

I'm not trying to force my way in. Of course they have a vendor who does what I do! Own that and play the long game. This approach doesn't put them on their heels, and it makes it more difficult to reject me outright.

BE CONSISTENT

Water cuts through rock because of its persistence. It keeps coming. Play the long game, like Ryan did. It's okay if you're told no 200 times.

The more seeds you plant, the more you'll harvest. Water the seeds. Be so visible they can't ignore you forever.

We live in a world where everyone wants success *yesterday*. But here's the truth—the winners you see out there? They've been panning for gold for years. They've been told *no* thousands of times. You wouldn't hit the gym four times and expect to come out looking like seven-time Mr. Olympia, Phil Heathe. So why the hell would prospecting be any different?

Show up. Do the work. Earn their respect. Stay consistent, and you'll earn their trust—and their business.

ADD VALUE

What would get your attention from a salesperson? How could they differentiate from all the others that contact you?

"Steve, it's Tom with [ABC] Company. I hit you up a few weeks ago and talked about building your bench and having a Plan B."

"What's up?"

"I shot you an email with a link to an article on marketing your General Contracting Company. There was some stuff in there that I thought was unique and wanted to send it your way. I called just to tell you to look for it in case it went to spam."

If you want to add real value to someone, stop overthinking it—meet a need, solve a problem, or make their life easier. Stack enough value, and you won't have to beg for business—you'll *be* the obvious choice.

Look, if your ideal client is a business owner, what are they dealing with? They want more profit. They hate wasting money on shit marketing. They've got employee headaches. Be the one who shows up with answers. Be a resource they can count on.

Everyone's asking, *"What's in it for me?"* Your job? Keep showing them why they need you in their circle.

I once had a contractor email me saying he got so much out of my stuff that he told his buddy to hire me. He couldn't hire me himself— he was retiring—but he still sent me business because I brought value.

Add value. Do the work. You never know when or where that gold's going to pan out.

BE YOUR OWN BIGGEST FAN

Here's the last condition for success I need to hammer home: I'm floored by how many business owners and salespeople aren't out there screaming from the rooftops about who they are and how they help.

Everyone *says* they're the best. Everyone *claims* they bring value. But when it's time to actually show the world? Crickets.

Shouting from the rooftops can mean pounding the pavement, meeting people face-to-face, or showing up loud and proud on social media. Go check your personal Facebook right now—if someone can't tell what you do with one glance of your profile bio, fix that today. And don't feed me that "I like to keep business and personal separate" crap. You're not running a Fortune 500 company. You're a small business hunting for attention, leads, and profit.

Be damn proud of what you do. Own it. Celebrate the value you bring. Stay authentic. Stay real. But get loud.

CHAPTER 13

SELLING UNAFRAID TO YOUR DATABASE

There's gold sitting right under your damn nose—just waiting for you to claim it.

Your database—yeah, that list of past clients, leads, and contacts— is a freaking goldmine. Call it a CRM; call it whatever you want… It's an organized pile of opportunity. There are tons of tools out there for this, and it doesn't take more than a quick Google search or asking around to find what works best for your industry.

But here's the deal: None of that matters if you're not using it *consistently*. This isn't optional. It's a non-negotiable standard if you're serious about winning.

Selling Unafraid to your database comes down to two things: hunting and farming. Hunting is chasing new opportunities. Farming is nurturing what you've already got. Both will make you a ton of money—if you quit dabbling and commit the time and resources to actually work the system.

During my first two years in business, I totally blew it with my database—primarily because I didn't have one. My system looked like one of these two scenarios:

Phone Rings with a Lead

___ Run the Sales Call
___ Sell & Complete the Job
___ Find the Next Client

or

Phone Rings with a Lead

___ Run the Sales Call
___ Don't Get the Job
___ Find the Next Client.

I had no idea I was supposed to keep their information or what I could do with it. I was just trying to find people who wanted what I did, and I thought anything more complicated than this was for bigger companies with deeper pockets.

This ignorance cost me at least $2 million in sales during the first three years of my business, so get off your ass. If you don't currently have a database, it's time to take action. If you do have one, pay close attention to this chapter and apply the insights you learn.

Viewing my database, I identify three distinct groups, each needing a distinct mix of hunting and farming to maximize profits:

PAST CLIENTS

This group is the lowest-hanging fruit and should get the bulk of your attention. The likelihood of making another sale to a past client ranges between 60% and 70%—or even higher, depending on their previous experiences with your company. In contrast, the probability of selling to a new prospect is between 5% and 20%, depending on the quality of the lead and the skill of the salesperson.

Once someone has given you money, they're more likely to do it again because they've already used you and are familiar with you and your brand. You've already come through for them before, and they believe you will again. Trust has already been established.

Unfortunately, many companies do a lousy job of keeping these relationships warm. This is where farming comes into play. Farm your past clients by staying on their radar. The more they think of you, the better the chance of a repeat sale or a referral. Stay in touch with regular emails that add value instead of always promoting a sale. Send tips and other content that meets the needs they're likely to have. When I implemented this in my painting company, it regularly generated 20-30 more projects a year.

Another farming activity is what I call the Warranty Call. Most companies run like an Olympic Gold Medal Sprinter when it comes to honoring warranties. Sure, they'll stand behind it if the client calls, but there's no way they'll go looking for warranty work. This is an opportunity to differentiate in your market.

Pick the phone up and say something like the following: "Hi Lee. It's Tom with ABC Decks. We built your deck last fall and your labor warranty is almost up. I wanted to schedule a visit to make sure everything is looking right so it doesn't become an issue later. How's next Thursday at 4:30 p.m.?"

Picture the goodwill you build just by showing up. They remember why they hired you in the first place. In my experience, about 30% of the time I went back for a warranty visit, the client would bring up another project they were thinking about—boom, more work on the calendar. That's the Law of Reciprocity in full swing. You give, they give back.

And if the thought of going back to review your work freaks you out, that's a red flag. If you're delivering a kickass product or service, there's nothing to be nervous about. Odds are, you'll just confirm you did great work and open the door for more.

I hunt my past client database like an absolute savage. Remember Bob the GC I told you about? The guy stacked an extra *million bucks* in revenue from one simple move. He used what we call the UIT—the *Unexpected Intentional Touch*. It's stupid simple, insanely powerful, and ridiculously profitable.

And I gotta give credit where it's due—shoutout to my coach, Ben Newman (who wrote the foreword for this book), for coining the term UIT. The dude's a machine, and this tactic flat-out works if you've got the stones to use it.

At one of my private workshops, I introduced this sales tactic to a company, and within an hour of applying it, they secured a $50k sale. By the next day, as I was flying out of town, they clinched another $30k. They basically began to shit money when they attacked what I taught.

Here, I'll outline the basics of this tactic and encourage you to try it for 90 days. Consistency is crucial.

A UIT is a straightforward method for salespeople to exploit profit opportunities right under their noses. Most don't keep their relationships with past clients warm. This tactic addresses that in just 10–15 minutes a day.

Here's how it works:

1. Select three past clients.
2. Pick up the phone or send each a personalized text message that says something like, *"Joe, it's Tom from [ABC] Company. We worked on your _____ last year/month. How's it going/looking? Let me know when you have a moment. I'd love to catch up."*

Don't pitch anything. You're simply showing you care about them and are curious how they're doing. Most companies sell their things and then go dark and impersonal. This is a differentiator.

Our KPIs indicate that roughly 5% of these interactions result in additional revenue over a year. Sending three messages a day over 260 working days totals 780 touches. (It's okay to contact the same individuals multiple times a year if your database is smaller.) Some may not respond, but others will engage.

From there, it's simply a matter of having a conversation that can lead to repeat business or referrals.

780 x 5% = 39 self-generated sales.

Multiply 39 by your average sale value, and you're looking at significant revenue.

Below are a few more examples. Keep them short. Make them yours. The reps you put in will eventually help you find the right messages that drive engagement and lead to sales conversations with clients eager for your assistance. I don't care what you sell. Make it a non-negotiable that your sales team implements this.

Example 1

> *"Katie. It's Tom from Titan Decks. We finished your deck last September, and I just wanted to connect with you and see how it's looking. When you get a minute, hit reply and let me know. Have a great day."*

Example 2

> *"Mike. It's Tom from Patriot Electric. It was great working with you last year. I was curious how those new lights we installed were performing for you. Hit me back when you have a few and fill me in."*

By proactively and intentionally reaching out, you will also uncover any issues they might be hesitant to mention, allowing you to provide better service and stand by your work. Often, they'll say, "Everything's great, but since you reached out, we were thinking of doing [XYZ]. Can you help with that?"

It's crucial that all your salespeople engage in this as a daily non-negotiable. I know I said that already, but it bears repeating: don't underestimate the power of prospecting your database of past clients.

DEAD LEADS

Regarding dead leads, I recently thought I had lost a sale for one of our programs. The negative self-talk was getting to me, with thoughts like *They lied to you and had no intention of joining* or *They probably think it's too much money.* That nasty negative self-talk almost got me, but I took action.

I sent a text to the prospect who had gone dark on me: *"Are you still interested in coaching?"* Within a minute, I received an apology for the delay in signing up, explaining that life issues had gotten in the way.

Life sometimes interrupts your prospects' ability to take action. I've had prospects go silent due to a death in the family, a new job, or other life events.

For these "dead" contacts, I employ various strategies. For example, *"Sam, it's Tom from [ABC] Company. We spoke last winter about _____. Did you ever go ahead with the project?"* This can sometimes revive the deal. People get distracted and may not have hired anyone. In fact, at the time of this writing, just yesterday I received a message from a woman named Karra apologizing for blowing me off a few months ago when we were discussing her painting project. She said "life happened" and wanted to hire my company, Simplify Painting to do her project. Her message was in response to a text I sent last week asking her if she ever did the project.

Recently, I challenged our BATTLEGROUND members to reach out to at least ten dead leads. A day later I got this: "Tom, this is Dave. I called eleven dead leads yesterday and sold a $160,000 project! They had some things going on in their life and it got pushed down the road. They thanked me for reaching out and are ready to go! LFG!"

Another approach is simply picking up the phone and asking for help: "Joe, we talked a while ago about doing that project for you. I'm calling because I need some help. I've got this button I need to click in my database to tell it where to put your file. It keeps popping up as a reminder. I need to move it to the 'Keep following up' file or the 'We're done' file. Which of those makes the most sense?"

It's okay to win a sale or lose one, but not knowing is unacceptable.

Don't make assumptions about why they've ghosted you and seem to have gone into the witness protection program. Do your part. Many will appreciate your follow-up, and you might find they still haven't hired anyone, even after months or even a year in Dave's case.

LEADS YOU NEVER HAD CONTACT WITH

For leads you've never had contact with—those who might have filled out a form on your website or provided their information in some other way—I keep them on my email list. I might send some direct mail. We might even pick up the phone and remind them that they reached out and that we're here if they want to talk.

What I want you to understand is that every segment of your database is important. Every segment presents opportunities for you and your team to *SELL UNAFRAID*. You just need to do the work.

A LITTLE ADDED MOTIVATION

What's your cost to acquire a new client? How about your cost per lead? What does it cost to lose a client? These are very real questions with very real answers that feed or deplete your bank account.

For example, if you spend $100,000 a year on marketing and generate 200 leads a year, your cost per lead is $500. You're dropping $500 bucks to get the phone to ring, regardless of the quality of that lead or the outcome.

$100,000 / 200 = $500 (cost per lead)

If your sales close rate is 40%, you'll sell 80 units of your thing. Your cost to acquire a customer is $1,250.

200 / 40% = 80 (units sold)

$100,000 (marketing spend) / 80 (units sold) = $1,250 (cost per lead)

I am all for investing in paid marketing and believe it should be a part of your attraction strategy, but when you start to look at the math, it just makes sense to hunt and farm the database you've already paid to build.

Take UITs as an example. Sending three a day will take an average of about 15 minutes. Anyone can do that. A total of 780 touches to past clients will return approximately 39 sales. Those 39 sales would cost you $48,750 to get based on the example math above. In comparison, 15 minutes a day over the course of 260 sales days is around 5 hours a month of a salesperson's time going after a segment that is 70% more likely to buy than those leads generated by paid advertising.

I realize some of you reading this might be thinking, *I get all of my sales from word of mouth. I don't spend anything on marketing.* Great! That's where we all want to be. But this still applies to you. You're already doing something amazing in the service and the experience you're providing. What would happen if you implemented UIT's? Warranty calls? Pour gas on the flame you already have burning.

Selling Unafraid will mean loving up on the people you've already sold. It will mean caring about those who ghosted you. It will mean taking a shot to engage the ones you never had contact with.

Engage your database regularly. I dare you.

CHAPTER 14
WINNING WITH YOUR NETWORK

W ho's standing in front of your ideal client every damn day? What other businesses are constantly rubbing shoulders with the people who *need* to know you? That's what I call an Influencer.

People love to say, *"It's not what you know, it's who you know."* Yeah, okay... but here's what's even stronger: *It's not who you know—it's who knows you exist.* If they don't know you're out there, you don't stand a chance.

Case in point—we recently had to fix our dryer. The thing was on life support. We were literally reaching into the drum, spinning it by hand, slamming the door shut, and praying to the appliance gods that it would fire up. The noises and cussing coming out of the Reber house during that routine? Comedy gold. But trust me, the struggle was real.

I went to Google and typed in *"dryer repair Colorado Springs."* I called one of the numbers and was greeted by a friendly voice. I explained our issue, and he said, "We just sell parts—we don't do repairs. I can sell you the kit you need to fix it and walk you through how to do it, or I can give you Tony's number, and he can take care of it."

I gladly took Tony's number and called him. He answered on the second ring with a positive vibe and gratitude that I reached out. I bring this up because that's exceptional. It's a sad reflection on the state of things that something as simple as a pleasant, positive greeting stands out as being extraordinary.

Tony said he could come out the next morning and even arrived a little early to get started. While he was here, he discovered another issue that required parts from the original guy I had contacted. These guys were helping each other grow their businesses.

Both have contact with people like me every day, and they both win.

Through similar relationships, I have sold millions of dollars in every business I've owned. This is a huge missed opportunity for salespeople in all industries.

When we were painting hundreds of homes a year, I knew I could count on Joel to be responsible for a couple of handfuls of those projects each year. As a Home Inspector, he walks into hundreds of homes each year, frequently being asked, "Do you know a ….?" The relationship I had with Joel was easily eight to ten projects every year, like clockwork.

Then there was Joe. He installed carpet. Another eight to ten jobs.

Adding in my realtor and designer network, we could stack another couple dozen or more projects to the mix.

We added about 100 new clients a year to our database through our influencer network. Consider the lifetime value of these clients when referrals and repeat business are factored in.

You'll see this happening all around you if you pay attention. The realtor has a lender. The lender has the appraiser. The tire store has the wheel repair shop.

What about you? Are you intentionally building your brand and sales through influencer relationships? If not, read on, and I'll tell you how.

THE 1-100 LIST

I had a goal to have 100 influencers tell the world about me. I knew that by building an influencer list and strengthening those relationships, the math could quickly grow. For example, if you have just ten solid influencers and they each referred you to someone once per quarter, that would be forty new leads. Our close rate on influencer leads always hovered around 90%.

Forty leads with a 90% close rate yield thirty-six new projects. Multiply that by your average sale size, and you can see how the revenue grows.

To build my list, I categorized potential influencers. For my painting company, I listed categories like Home Inspector, Remodeler, Plumber, Electrician, Roofer, Realtor, and Interior Designer, among others. In The Contractor Fight, we have influencers specializing in marketing for contractors, those who have created powerful CRMs for the construction industry, and others who sell construction products to contractors who need our services.

Once my list of categories was created, I listed these categories down the left side of a piece of paper. On the right, I drew a table with three columns, aiming to have three influencers in each category. Then, I filled in the slots of the relationships I already had, leaving the open spaces as targets to fill.

Most salespeople handle this without any difficulty. They typically fall apart on the implementation. First, they say they don't have time. As I covered earlier, this is BS: there's always time. It doesn't take much. Next, they don't implement it because they don't know what to say. Not knowing what to say is understandable when you're new at something. I get it. You don't want to look stupid, say the wrong thing, shoot yourself in the foot. But, again, it was covered earlier; just keep it simple and have fun with it. You won't be perfect, but you will get better over time and find what works best for you. Remember, as long as we work to get better, we will never be as bad at something as we were in the beginning!

"I see you do interior design. I do hardwood floors, and I thought we might want to get to know each other."

"I sell appliance parts and thought we could help each other since you do the actual repairs. Is it crazy for us to have a conversation?"

Make your list and start reaching out a couple of times a day.

Social media is another way to connect with possible influencers. Follow accounts that you want to learn more about. Comment on their posts and add value. Share resources that will benefit them. Send a referral now and then, and tell them who you referred to them. The more value you add, the more you get on their radar as a person of value.

Finally, there are numerous business networking groups in your area. Join one. Add value, and you'll get value in return.

Your influencers, like you, want more business. They're looking for an edge. They want higher sales, higher profits, and anything else that will ease their stress as a salesperson or business owner.

Once I've built my list, I stay in touch. As with the UITs I talked about, send a couple of influencer touches a day that make their life easier or solve a problem. For example, you can send them this book! Send them a link to an article that helps them in their business. Invite them to an event and pay their way. When they connect you with someone, send a thank you gift or a note expressing your gratitude.

Finally, I often get asked how my influencers are compensated. In my experience, most don't want anything other than for their clients to have an amazing experience as they work with you. Most of mine were happy for me to treat them to a beer or coffee a couple of times a year. Yours may want a finders fee. I never asked for money when I referred because I wanted to keep things simple. Who knows what yours will want? Have those conversations upfront and keep communicating with them.

Building your influencer network, just like prospecting for new clients, will take time and consistency, but in the end, it will grow your profits. There are free and highly qualified leads waiting for you when you commit to this.

PART 4
BEYOND THE SALE

CHAPTER 15

DO YOU STILL CARE ABOUT ME?

The Queen and I love each other every day. We encourage each other, stay connected, touch, talk—all of it. Why wouldn't we? We're married! We met, dated, worked our asses off to impress each other, and finally closed the deal at what ended up being our second-choice wedding venue.

And here's where most couples blow it—after the deal is sealed, they get lazy.

Salespeople do the same thing. We land the client, then coast. We court the prospect, making them feel important. We return calls immediately when we're trying to make the sale and go out of our way to earn their trust and business. Then, once the deal is closed, we move on to the next one, repeating the process. Companies in every industry bust their tails and spend millions to get new clients while shoving their existing clients to the back of the line.

I don't believe we do this intentionally. We don't wake up thinking, *Today, I'm going to give my clients my scraps.* We simply get caught up in the chase for new leads, and unless we're intentional about it, we neglect the people who have already proven they trust us. We assume that because they hired us once, they will do so again. Without consistent care and nurturing, they will feel like they're not important and just had a one-night stand with your company.

I consistently work hard to make Lee feel important, and she does the same for me because we want our relationship to grow stronger over time, not weaker.

How are you doing in this area with your clients—scale of 1 to 10? Be brutally honest. And don't you dare pick "7." You and I both know 7 is the coward's number. Nobody gets fired up about 7.

I've hired a ton of companies over the years for all kinds of things, and one of my biggest disappointments? After the sale, after the work was done—radio silence. Nothing. Like I never existed.

And I'll be real with you—a while back, we caught ourselves doing the same thing in The Contractor Fight. Yeah, we've got an awesome, tight-knit coaching community, but we were screwing up. We didn't have a system to make our members feel like rock stars. All eyes were on growing membership, and in the process, we were taking the people who already trusted us for granted. The second we saw it, we made changes—fast. We'll talk about that in a bit.

But let's zoom out. You bought this book because you want to grow your business, serve more people, and make more money—and damn right, you should. One of the fastest ways to grow is to keep the clients you've already got.

Keith Cunningham, one of the smartest business minds out there, asked a question that punched me right in the face: *"How big would your business be if you still had every customer who ever tried you?"*

Let that sink in. What if every single person who ever bought a car from you bought *every* car from you for life? What if every time someone wanted their house painted, *you* were their guy—no questions asked?

One of the biggest killers in business is losing repeat customers and not being referred like clockwork. Fix that, and your business will explode.

Here are some eye-opening statistics:[1]

- The average company loses between 10% and 25% of its customers each year.

---

1. Zippia, "28 Critical Customer Retention Statistics: Average Customer Retention Rate By Industry," January 16th, 2023, zippia.com

- By increasing customer retention rates by just 5%, companies can boost their profits by up to 95%.
- Only 18% of businesses prioritize customer retention over customer acquisition.
- Companies have a 60%–70% chance of selling to an existing customer versus a 5%–20% chance of selling to a new customer.
- 65% of a company's business comes from existing customers.
- It costs 6 to 7 times more to acquire new customers than to retain existing ones.

Making the sale shouldn't mark the end of your courtship of your clients. What would happen to your profits if you made "loving them" your top business growth strategy? When we realized we could significantly improve by intentionally showing our clients we care about them, we took action. That's when I implemented UITs.

As the founder, I wanted these to come directly from me. They're not automated or sent in bulk. Typically, I send them via text or a video message. A simple, *"Joe, it's Tom from The Fight. You've been in the program for a few weeks, and I wanted to check in and see how you're doing. Hit me back when you can and let me know."*

The amount of information I receive about our clients is staggering. I hear about business struggles, family issues, and health problems. This allows me to look into how we can help them through whatever they're experiencing. I get it—running a coaching business makes it easier to build deep personal connections. That's baked into what we do. But, you can apply this same mindset in *any* business.

I also know that as the company grows, I can't personally handle every single touchpoint. That's reality. But that doesn't give us a pass. It means we've got to build a process—a system—so nobody slips through the cracks. No excuses. Every client should feel seen, valued, and important, whether I'm the one reaching out or someone on my team is doing it.

Another thing we implemented was a kickass onboarding process for our new clients. Over their first 90 days, in addition to our regular coaching calls, we added six small group calls for new members and provided them with a map to follow. We connect with them, answer questions, and help them solve their problems immediately. We aim for quick wins.

Finally, we hired Aaron. He is our Member Champion for the community. He loves people and loves to serve. His job is to connect with our clients, and when he identifies needs, he connects them with the right resource—be it a coach or fellow member—to get them the help they need. You can find him encouraging people, connecting people, and, most importantly, loving people on a daily basis.

These focused actions have improved client retention in just a few short months. I have also set a crazy goal for client retention in The Fight: zero members leaving. As I say, it's crazy and highly unlikely that we'll actually hit it, but setting the target as "nobody leaves" has caused our team to level up and consistently bring our best. A new standard for all of us.

How would you and your team show up if you had a "never lose a client" mentality? How would that impact how quickly you answered the phone? The experience you provided through every sale? Your approach to UITs? Setting a standard like this would position you as exceptional in your industry. Exceptional wins. At this point, I hope you're all-in when it comes to intentionally showing your clients you still care about them. Now, let's get tactical and discuss a few ways to implement your new standard.

THE WARRANTY CALL

Yes, we covered this in an earlier chapter. However, it's low-hanging fruit from a retention point of view. You pick up the phone—yes, the phone—and talk to them. No sales pitch. No agenda other than "We want to make sure everything's still cool and get ahead of any problems so you don't need to deal with them." They hired you and—if you're implementing what I've suggested in this book—paid a premium to do so. Part of the deal is hunting for problems *before* your client finds them. Your job is to find the little issues and fix them so they're not piling up more crap on their already overloaded to-do list. That's how you stand out. That's how you become their go-to.

WARRANTY RESPONSE TIME

Your phone rings; a client tells you about an issue they're having. How quickly do you get it taken care of? The correct answer is "Yesterday." Many companies drag their feet when it comes to issues or callbacks to address their clients' problems. Currently, we employ a mosquito control company. Their deal is that if mosquitos are an issue after their monthly application, they will come back out at no charge and reapply the bug juice.

Here's the problem: when I call a few days after the application and say, "The mosquitoes are back, and they're pissed off," the reply I get is, "We try to schedule the reapplication within seven days." That's several more days that I'm being run out of our gorgeous backyard, unable to enjoy it. Mother Nature in Colorado is a bat-shit-crazy-bitch, and we only get so many nights a year out there. Now, they're robbing me of more. That's unacceptable and illustrates their lack of appreciation for me as a customer. I even told them to charge me more if it meant getting them out the next day—crickets. I'm still waiting at least a week. Finding a new company is now on my to-do list.

UNEXPECTED INTENTIONAL TOUCHES (UIT'S)

I've shared enough on these; hopefully, you get the point. This is ridiculously simple. Do them.

Client Appreciation Party

Throw a bash every year and invite all your clients. Feed them and just have a good time. Again, no pitch. No agenda other than showing appreciation and reinforcing that you still care. One of our clients, who owns a landscape design company, partnered with another business owner who runs a high-end audio-visual business—the type that installs amazing sound systems, TVs, and home theaters. They serve similar clientele and pool their resources to host a party annually. This party not only creates community but also boosts sales for both companies, thanks to the conversations that clients have with each other.

Gifting

The FedEx dude knocked on my door and handed me a package. I had no idea what it was or who it was from. Since it was addressed to Lee and me, I asked her to come into the kitchen and open it with me. Inside was a set of wine glasses and a cutting board engraved with our initials, T & L. Logan Shinholser owns Contractor Growth Network, a contractor marketing company, and our company often refers clients to him. Logan knows we like to have our own little happy hour now and then, with a nice Sancerre and Triscuits with pepper jack cheese. He reached out to Giftology, an amazing company that helps you send the right gifts to people that matter and shared a bit about us with John Ruhlin's team. (John is the founder of Giftology, and in his book of the same name, he makes a strong case for the power of gifting.)

We use this gift several times a month and think of Logan every time we do.

Handwritten Notes

Is anyone else sick of getting bills or car warranty promotions in the mail? Me too! Grab a pen and a blank notecard or company stationary and drop a quick note in the mail. Thank them. Wish them a happy birthday. Write something other than "hire me" and make sure it brightens their day.

Uncommon effort leads to uncommon results.

Do you still care about me? Am I still important to you? This is rolling around somewhere in the minds of your clients. Do your part: give them 100% and let the rest fall into place.

CHAPTER 16
MIND THE GAP

If you've been to London, you've seen the signs: *"Mind the Gap."* I first heard the phrase over 25 years ago when a woman's voice came over the speaker system while I rode the Underground or the Tube—our version of the subway. "Mind the Gap," she said, making sure we didn't stick our feet between the train car and the platform.

Mind the Gap is a version of "watch your step," as we say in the United States. Watch your step, or you'll trip. Watch your step, or you fall on your face. Mind the Gap, or trouble will show itself.

In business, there's a gap between when you make the sale and when you deliver on it. This gap could be a day, a few weeks, or a year. This gap is often a place where sales go to die. It's no man's land. It can be a silent and confusing place for your new client to be. This gap is where assumptions are made, and problems grow.

Many years ago, I worked with a contractor named Mike. He shared that he would often sell a job, and then, when he reached out to schedule it, he found out they already had the work done. They'd say things like, "We thought you forgot about us," or "It had been a few weeks since we heard from you, so we hired someone else." We did some math and realized Mike was dropping the ball on over $100k of sales a year with this one oversight.

This is "friendly fire": the kind of damage you inflict on yourself unintentionally.

As a consumer, I feel I've spent a lifetime chasing down businesses, wondering what the hell is happening next. "When are you coming?" "You said you'd send the paperwork after I said yes—where is it?"

When I'm left in the dark, wondering what's next, my mind starts writing its own stories—and they're usually worst-case scenarios.

My stories are seldom true and usually have a negative ring to them. "They don't care." "Typical sales guy." "Thanks for adding something to my to-do list."

When we're finalizing a sale, we make promises like "Our company is different," "We put you first," and "You're paying more for the value we deliver."

And then we act like every other company they've had experiences with in the past. Average. Mediocre. Shitty.

Minding the gap—staying on top of communication—will save your ass from a couple of big problems down the road.

First up: buyer's remorse. That sinking feeling people get after the high of making a purchase fades, and reality kicks in. Here's the truth —the real work to win over your clients *starts* after the paperwork is signed. That's when trust is either built or shattered. If you made promises during the sale and then fumble the follow-through, you're basically telling them, *"Yeah... you made a bad call."* Don't be that guy.

For example, after I sell a project, I tell the client what was going to happen and when it would happen.

"Joe, I'm excited to move ahead on the project. Here's what happens now. I send this information to my Project Manager, who handles the scheduling. He will review the details and pick my brain with any questions. Then, he will assign it to the crew leader best suited for the job. Once that happens, he will call you to nail down an exact start date for the job. You will get this call within 48 hours from now. After he calls you, you will hear from our crew leader about a week prior to your start date. He will ask to set a time to walk the job with you and make sure nothing has changed, and also so he understands any concerns you might have."

This sets the table for a great experience. Our job is to do everything, just like I said. When we do, we are showing the client that they made a great choice.

Next, minding the gap will reduce confusion and chaos. Your customers don't do what you do every day. To you, the thing you do is routine because you do it hundreds of times a year. To them, it can be overwhelming. The sale continues after the sale with the experience we provide. Do what you can to personalize their experience and create order. Ask them—yes, ask them—what they need from you to have clarity about what's happening.

Remember the "make me feel important" stuff we covered earlier? It applies here, too. Do what you can to roll out the red carpet every step of the way for your clients. Take some time to pick up the phone and ask how they're feeling about things.

Let's pretend you've communicated that the delivery of something they purchased was delayed again. You let them know and move on with your day. Consider picking up the phone a day or two later to check in. "Mary, I know I called the other day and gave you the news on the delivery. I understand that things like this can be disappointing, and I wanted to ask how you're doing with it. Is there anything I can do at the moment?"

Taking some extra time not only to communicate the information but also to give them a chance to "be heard" goes a long way in how they feel. They might be clear on what's happening but make no assumptions that they're feeling important.

During COVID, we ordered a pool table. We were told it would be delivered in three months. We were a little bummed, but we understood that delays happen and said, "No problem."

The pool table was installed a year later.

The installers were great, and the table is great, but the experience sucked. We initiated every bit of contact with the company for a year. Every time the next promised deadline approached, we hoped for an update and never got one unless we called. The only way we ever knew what was happening was by chasing down our sales guy—who, for the record, didn't seem to give a crap once we ordered and paid for the table. We felt like a pain in their ass instead of a valued customer.

Imagine how you'd set your company apart from all others if you provided a concierge-type experience. What would that look like for you? Picture an experience where they were never in the dark about where things stood.

What would it take for them to say, "This was the best experience I've ever had with a company"?

CHAPTER 17
BOOST PROFITS WITH SOCIAL MEDIA

O n Valentine's Day, 2008, I created my Facebook account. At the time, I had no idea how powerful this and other social media platforms would be to my businesses. I remember thinking, *How are we going to sell paint jobs on this thing?*

Over the past 15 years, I've learned a ton about social media—and I'm still learning, still testing, still dialing it in. I've sold millions of dollars in services through these platforms and helped others collectively sell hundreds of millions using simple, no-BS strategies.

Most small businesses? They're ghosts on social media. Yeah, they've got accounts. They post here and there. Maybe stumble into a sale once in a while—like a blind squirrel finding a nut. But that's not a plan.

In this chapter, I'm going to share what's actually worked for me—stuff you can take, tweak, and make your own. I also lump podcasting into social media because it builds community and trust, and you can chop up the content and spray it across other platforms to keep eyeballs on you.

Look—I know I can't speak to every single challenge you face, especially if you're in an industry with dumb social media regulations tying your hands. Do what you can with what I give you.

At the time I'm writing this, I've cranked out over 1,000 podcast episodes, more than 1,500 YouTube videos, and thousands of posts across Facebook, Instagram, LinkedIn, and TikTok. The one thing I've nailed? Building community. Getting real engagement. That builds trust—and trust builds sales.

Before we dive in, I need to hit on something I see all the time: business owners who refuse to post on their personal profiles because they "don't want to mix business and personal." That's garbage. People buy from people. They don't care about logos or fancy company names—they care about who *you* are. The business owners who show up, who let people in on their lives, their beliefs, their values… those are the ones who sell more. Every time.

Here are five things I've learned that keep ringing the cash register:

1. Show Us Your Life

You are your brand. People are choosing *you*—not just your product or service. Show us your family. Show us the fire that drives you. Where did it come from? Let us in.

I was at an event once, and the host told me he wanted to be the "Gary Vee" of his industry. I looked him in the eye and said, "Why not just be *you*?" You've got a good family, a good business—give people *that*.

It's easy to copy what the big names are doing, but don't lose who you are in the process. The people who make the biggest impact don't just share highlight reels—they show the bloopers too. I've been open about my struggles with infertility, bankruptcy, and the garbage self-talk I've had to fight. That's what makes people connect.

2. Get Social

The word "social" is in *social media* for a reason. Engage. Don't just post garbage graphics that say "Hire Us! Call Now!" and expect magic to happen. You've got to talk to people. Start conversations.

3. Tell Stories

Humans have told stories for thousands of years. Stories connect. Stories sell. Most companies suck at this. It doesn't matter if you paint houses or sell software—master the art of storytelling, and you'll separate yourself from the noise.

4. Make People Pick a Side

I show up on social media to make people take a stance. Either I'm their kind of guy or I'm not. I'm good with either outcome. People respect authenticity and want to work with people who stand for something.

5. Look for Stories in Your Everyday Life

In November 2022, I ran a private workshop in Vancouver. As Lee and I sat on the plane just before takeoff, I posted a selfie and shared a little about how I roll. Most people would've snapped a cliché plane selfie with some cheesy caption, like "Headed to speak to some entrepreneurs." Not me. I look for stories in everyday moments—and that's what I post.

Here's exactly what I wrote in that post…

SHE COMES WITH ME

I travel quite a bit for the work I do.

I travel to give Keynotes, Sales Training, and Leadership Workshops and occasionally to work one-on-one with my clients. I help high performers take it higher.

I like to travel, but it screws up our routine at home. A one-day workshop impacts at least three days of our life with travel days.

If you travel enough, those days away stack into weeks and sometimes months away each year.

Today, we're headed to Vancouver, BC, for a workshop I'm doing.

Someone asked me recently why she travels with me. Most men can't wait to hit the road & get away. Most men don't bring their wives almost EVERY TIME they travel. This guy took notice.

I understand that some have younger kids, and the spouse needs to stay home. I understand many couples have a sick relative to care for. Or, maybe she has a career and can't get away. Fair enough. I get it. There are a few valid reasons why some couples can't do it the way we do it.

But… that's not most couples.

When he asked me, "I notice The Queen travels with you to all the events you do. What's with that?" I replied, "I am not willing to spend one more night away than needed from her and our groove and our routine. When we're apart, our communication isn't as smooth. When we're apart, our power and impact is limited. The right 1 + 1 = 3. She comes first. This is non-negotiable."

Men: show her she's YOUR priority. Show her that she is crucial to your success and for you having your "mojo" dialed in. Show her that it matters that she is WITH you.

Send a message to anyone watching: this is what a great relationship looks like. The world needs more good examples.

If you find yourself looking forward to getting away from her on a regular basis, call a time-out and figure out your relationship.

If you travel, take some time and find a way to make it happen for her to be with you. Put in the effort. It's worth it. Building your business or career is far less important than building your marriage. Your career will be better when your marriage is stronger. Success starts at home.

All I know is when you see me speaking and coaching around the country, there's a massive chance that My Queen is on my hip.

There was no pitch. Nothing about joining our program or hiring me for a workshop. Those things happen organically as I consistently tell stories. This post generated tens of thousands of revenue in a couple week period because I showed them who I was. In my work, I emphasize the importance of building a strong you, a strong home, and a strong business. This approach shows rather than tells.

This applies to showing your team and the culture you're building as well. Post about anything that humanizes you. Tell those stories and connect with your clients.

1. Be Where Your Ideal Clients Are Every Day

"Tom, what platforms should I be on?"

"The ones where your clients and potential clients are."

I'm on all the platforms I mentioned earlier because that's where my customers are. Your sales and profits are directly related to your ability to attract eyeballs and stay on their radar, even after you've made the sale. I believe in daily posting—numerous times—across multiple platforms. This is part of the marketing game in 2024. Accept it and take action. Hire a videographer. Hire a virtual assistant to help you post and manage everything that needs your attention. Document your day. A good editor can craft a compelling story.

My goal is for anyone who needs to know who I am to see me every time they open their phone. Commit to being omnipresent. I often hear people say, "I don't want to post too much." You can't post too much. Most posts have limited reach, so just commit to being consistent and show up daily to figure it out as you go.

That whole "figure it out as you go" thing—that's for all of you who overthink every damn move and won't do a thing unless it's perfect. Knock it off. That's stupid.

Crank out content on every platform you can. Post. Test. Adjust. Repeat. You're not launching a fucking space shuttle—you're just putting yourself out there. Stop stressing. Hit record. Hit post. Learn as you go. The ones who win are the ones who *move*.

Want a good laugh?
I've included a link to my first
YouTube video from 2014
as part of your free bonus for
purchasing this book:

It was the first step in a journey that has allowed me to build a few multi-million dollar companies, land a gig as an HGTV Host, and, most importantly, positively impact hundreds of thousands of lives. It was terrible. I looked like I was twelve. The sound and lighting were bad. But, I started.

One strategy I swear by—go live on whatever platform your clients hang out on. Hitting that "Go Live" button strips away the pressure to be perfect and forces you to just be you. Hop on, teach us something, do an "Ask Me Anything" about your industry, or rant a little about what drives you nuts in your field. Show some fire. It won't take long before you get comfortable on camera and start showing up unapologetically real. That's when people connect.

And if you're sitting there thinking, "What the hell do I post?"—stop overcomplicating it. Get out of your own head and think like your customer, not like the seller. Before you hit record or write that post, ask yourself:

- Who do I serve?
- What headaches do they deal with all the time?
- What questions do they keep asking about my industry?
- What complaints do they have that nobody's addressing?
- What pisses me off about my industry?

And, ditch the industry jargon. Speak in plain language that your ideal client actually uses and understands.

My buddy Micah Miller owns Easton Outdoors, a landscaping company out in Poquoson, Virginia. Since 2018, Micah's been steadily grinding, building his brand on social media. He struggled early on, just like we all do. He'd ask himself, "Why the hell am I even doing this?"

But he stuck with it—and it's paying off big time.

To his credit, he saw where the hockey puck was headed, not where it was presently, to paraphrase Wayne Gretzky. He stayed with it and, over the years, has experienced over 3x topline revenue growth and 7x net profit growth. Last year, his total marketing spend was only 1.6% of revenue. In addition to growing his company by millions, social media produced other benefits, as he shared with me in a text conversation last summer. I asked him, "What benefits have you experienced as a result of what you've done on social media?"

He responded:

"When I show up, I'm trusted. I don't have to explain who I am or why I'm the expert. I do this by sending a YouTube video ahead of myself that is directly related to the type of project they are looking for.

Anytime I make a post on my personal page that we need to add another team member, I have at least a dozen qualified applicants.

The team upsells seven out of ten jobs we visit because our clients watch our social. After I pick up the deposit check, I encourage our clients to follow us on social media and think about the projects they see, especially if there's anything else they'd like to add. When go-time comes to start the job, they almost always add more.

Local contractors send me referrals and clients. We interact with their pages, and they learn to trust us as well. When something is outside of their league or a client is a good fit for us, we are top of mind for them as well."

2. Take a Stand

Stop trying to be everything to everyone. This approach is killing your sales, and it's exhausting. In The Contractor Fight, we emphasize a few foundational concepts around which I create content. These are the principles I firmly stand by. Some people dismiss them as BS, listing all the reasons why they believe I'm full of shit. Others fully lean into this stuff—they grab it with both hands and run—and they preach it loud because it's completely changed their lives.

One of those game-changing concepts I hammer on is telling home improvement contractors to stop playing small and aim for at least a 50% gross profit. This means if it costs you $1 to do something, you should charge your client at least $2. There are many reasons why this makes sense—I won't go into them all here. The point is that it's uncommon in the trades and also one reason we have improved many contractors' lives worldwide. We plant our flag unapologetically and share countless stories of individuals who have revolutionized their financial situations by having the guts to charge what they're truly worth. There are hundreds of videos and podcasts that hammer this mindset home on our platforms.

Where do you need to take a stand? What unique approaches do you take with your services that might ruffle some feathers?

You don't need everyone; you just need the right few who respect you and get where you're coming from. Consistently producing content that educates your audience on these polarizing strategies will, over time, strengthen your brand, establish you as the expert, and increase your profits.

3. Be Seen Doing What You Want More Of

One of the biggest reasons people don't get sales from social media? Nobody knows what the hell you do. And they don't know because *you're not showing them.*

For example, one way I make a living is speaking. If I want more speaking gigs, the best thing I can do is to... show myself *speaking.* Share the behind-the-scenes stuff—like the time the power went out mid-talk, or when I got thrown a curveball 20 minutes before stepping on stage. How did I handle it? What did I feel at that moment? What adjustments did I make? I can also show others how I prepare for a talk, and give tips others can use in their own world.

For example, a video like this would add value to people who speak:

"What's up, guys? It's Tom. A lot of you know I speak for a living and have had the honor to stand on stages in front of thousands of people. But here's the thing—you're a speaker too. Maybe not on a big stage, but you speak to your team, your networking group, and your clients. So I wanted to share three things I do before every talk to make sure I show up with confidence and influence the room the way I want."

Then, I could drop those three tips. Share the real stuff. Let people in. Show them what I do—don't just *tell* them.

Want to sell more bathroom remodeling projects? Show how your team is doing the demo or installing the new vanity.

Over time, you will be known as the person who does that thing. Your name will become synonymous with what you do.

4. Be Consistent

One thing I absolutely nailed when building The Contractor Fight was pumping out a ton of content—and doing it *consistently*. I'm a big believer that putting out massive amounts of *good-enough* content will beat waiting around for the "perfect" post every time. Perfection only comes after tons of reps.

I launched my podcast on February 11, 2015. Since then, I've posted something—a podcast, YouTube video, or social media post—every single day for 3,555 days straight (at the time I'm writing this). Some day, it's five to ten pieces of content. Some days 20-25. Were those first posts polished? Hell no. But I kept showing up, kept swinging, and got better.

I talk to business owners all the time who whine that social media "doesn't work" for them. So I ask, *"How often are you posting?"*

"Once a week."

"A couple times a month."

That's not commitment. That's dabbling.

You can't win if you're not showing up in people's feeds on the regular. Stop being a hobbyist when it comes to building your brand.

Let's play a little game. Think of a laundry detergent. Odds are, you just thought of Tide. Why? Because they never stop running commercials. I'm 55 years old, and I can't remember a time I wasn't seeing a Tide commercial.

Your posts are mini-commercials for *you*. You've got to stay top of mind in your market.

No matter where you're at in your social media game, crank it up. Show us your life. Be where your ideal clients are. Take a stand. Be seen doing the stuff you want to be hired for. And most of all—show up *every single day* without compromise.

CONCLUSION
THE INTENT TO IMPLEMENT

Inaction is the killer. It's the one thing standing between you and Selling Unafraid—between you and every goal you've set.

We're drowning in information—books, podcasts, YouTube videos, Facebook groups, events—it's all right there. So why do only about 20% of people actually hit their goals?

The answer: *The Do.*

The doing is all that matters. Your intentions? Your vision boards? Your fancy plans? All worthless without execution.

Setting goals is fun. It's fresh, it's exciting, you feel like a badass writing it all down. But then you get punched in the face—and as Mike Tyson said, "Everybody has a plan until they get punched in the face."

Life's going to swing on you. Employees quit. Sales dry up. Clients complain. The economy shifts. Family drama hits. The question is: what do you do next? That response is where winners are made.

I've been punched in the face more times than I can count, and here are a few hard-earned lessons that'll help you keep moving forward and Selling Unafraid:

1. Expect the Punch

This isn't about walking around paranoid, waiting for disaster. It's about understanding that adversity is part of the deal. Be optimistic, but stay realistic.

Fill your pipeline constantly.

Role-play those objections.

Work on yourself daily.

When the punch comes—and they will—you'll be ready.

2. Set Your High-Level Code of Conduct

Get clear on what you want, reverse-engineer the daily actions to get there, and commit without compromise.

In The Fight, we call it living The FW Day—*Fucking Winner* mode, every damn day.

The FW Day is built around three Ps: **Personal, Pipeline, and Profit.**

Personal (2 things):

- Look at your goals.
- Get a workout in.

Pipeline (1 thing):

- Send three UIT's to past clients and at least one prospecting message to an influencer.

Profit (1 thing):

- Do something that protects or grows your profit today. Here are a few examples:
  - Pre-job cost a project before you send the quote.
  - Job-cost your last job and learn from it.
  - Send the invoice.

- Run a pre-job meeting to transfer trust and align your team.
- Train your team.
- Have the hard conversation you've been avoiding.
- Read, listen, or watch something that fuels your growth.
- Engage in a sales role-play.
- Seek out coaching.

Stack enough of these FW Days, and you'll create unstoppable momentum. Weeks turn into months. Your mindset hardens. Your bank account grows. And you become a damn machine.

SURROUND YOURSELF WITH WINNERS

Most people won't operate at the level I've laid out in this book. They're comfortable. They lack discipline. They play the victim.

But here's the truth—your environment will make or break you. You've got to surround yourself with killers—people chasing greatness, not excuses. That might mean cutting ties with old friends who hold you back. It might mean changing jobs, dialing back time with certain family members, or writing a check to join a mastermind or community that'll push you and hold your feet to the fire.

You're not alone—unless you choose to be. There are people out there grinding, leveling up, and eager to pull others up with them. But you've got to step into that circle.

You finished this book—hell yeah, congrats, and thank you. But now what? Is this going to be another thing you read, nodded along with, and shelved? Or are you going to get after it, apply what hit home for you, and cash in on that elite mindset?

It's all on you now.

Go *SELL UNAFRAID.*

THANK YOU FOR READING MY BOOK!

I appreciate your interest in my book and value your feedback as it helps me improve future versions of this book. I would appreciate it if you could leave your invaluable review on Amazon.com with your feedback. Thank you!

www.ingramcontent.com/pod-product-compliance
Lightning Source LLC
Chambersburg PA
CBHW072155090426
42740CB00012B/2270